Praise for the 1st edition

      The Legal English Manual is a fantastic reference guide for those seeking to elevate their use of English in a professional law-related context. The book is concise and extremely user-friendly, while providing a wealth of guidance for numerous practice scenarios. And it can add value to everyone from the law student to the seasoned lawyer.

Toni Jaeger-Fine | Assistant Dean | Fordham Law School (New York City)

      In today's international legal practice, working in English is inescapable but can be challenging for those who are not native speakers of English. This is where the Legal English Manual becomes a valuable resource. It provides users with a well-structured reference to commonly used terms in various areas of practice, as well as guides for written and oral communication. I fully recommend this for any lawyer who works in English!

Joel Lee | Associate Professor | Faculty of Law National University of Singapore

      This book provides the essence of the professional legal English language: professional language, legal terminology, and examples on how to use them in practical situations. It is hence more than a reference book for international law students and lawyers. Sample documents, checklists, and guidance for practical situations make this handbook a compass for international legal practice.

Larry Teply | Professor in Law, Creighton University, Nebraska (USA)
Chairman of the International Negotiation Competition for
Author of "Legal Negotiation in a Nutshell"

      The Legal English Manual, with its fresh approach and engaging content, is a very resource in maintaining and strengthening clear, accurate, and relevant communication in law.

Frank Astill | President, International Negotiation Competition for Law Students
Former Director of The University of Sydney Law Extension Committee (Australia)

      This is a valuable manual for non-native speakers to improve their legal writing and speaking skills! It contains lots of useful terminology, phrases, and tips in a well-organized style which makes it easy for users to find the information they need easily.

Tetsuo Morishita | Professor | Sophia University Law School, Tokyo (Japan)

Praise for the 1st edition

66 *The Legal English Manual is so much more than the title suggests; it contextualizes the use of legal English so that students and practitioners can use the lessons for everything from getting a job to retaining and communicating with clients to advocating and negotiating on behalf of those clients. This book packs a huge educational punch into a highly efficient and user-friendly small package!* 99

Nancy Schultz | Professor of Law | Fowler School of Law
Chapman University, California (USA)

66 *With its clear explanation of legal vocabulary and useful form documents for both the U.S. and the U.K., this book is both an essential resource for civil-law lawyers, and an excellent guide for U.S. or U.K. lawyers who want to master the subtle differences in legal vocabulary and written forms between the two countries and their legal systems.* 99

John B. Thornton | Clinical Associate Professor of Law, Northwestern Pritzker School of Law, Chicago (USA) | Chair of the Section on Graduate Programs for Non-U.S. Lawyers of the American Association of Law Schools | Author of U.S. Legal Reasoning, Writing, and Practice for International Lawyers, Carolina Academic Press, 2014

66 *An excellent handbook providing students with an accurate, clear, and practice-oriented insight into all relevant Legal Skills issues.* 99
Stefano Troiano | Full Professor of Private Law | University of Verona (Italy)

66 *The Legal English Manual provides an exceptional overview of the various modes and styles of legal English communication. It provides key vocabulary terms for multiple practice areas, guidelines for different styles of legal writing, and advice for effective oral communication. Significantly, it places legal terminology into context, rather than simply providing isolated definitions. At the same time, it provides an appropriate depth of information without overwhelming the reader. Overall, it is a solid primer that will provide legal professionals anywhere in the world with the foundation they need to begin effectively communicating with other English-speaking professionals.* 99

Aaron Richard Harmon | B.A., M.A., J.D., LEED® AP
Clinical Assistant Professor | College of Law, Qatar University (Doha-Qatar)

Weston Walsh
Cornelius
Bollag
Kuhn-Schulthess
Wiebalck
Norman
von Zedtwitz

The Legal English Manual
2nd Edition

The Legal English Manual

2nd Edition

Handbook for Professional Legal Language
and Practical Skills

Kathrin Weston Walsh (Editor)
J.D., M.A. (Duke University School of Law)
Attorney (District of Columbia and Colorado)

Julian Cornelius
LL.B (Griffith College Dublin), LL.M. (University College Dublin)
Attorney (New York), Solicitor (Ireland, England, and Wales), Mediator

Jenna Bollag
BA LL.B (Monash University, Melbourne)
Lawyer (Supreme Court of Victoria, Australia)

Sandra Kuhn-Schulthess
Master's of Law (University of St. Gallen)
MAS in Customer Relationship Management (ZHAW Winterthur)

Alison Wiebalck
Dr. iur., BA LL.B (Macquarie University, Sydney)
Lawyer-Linguist in Zurich

Richard Norman
LL.M. (London)
Solicitor of the Supreme Court (England and Wales)

Clemens von Zedtwitz
Dr. iur., LL.M. (University of California, Los Angeles)
Rechtsanwalt in Zurich

in cooperation with:

BarWrite® Press

Published by
Lawbility Ltd., Sumatrastrasse 25, 8006 Zurich
Switzerland
www.lawbility.com

Co-published by
Verlag C.H.Beck oHG, Wilhelmstrasse 9, 80801 Munich
Germany
www.beck.de

Helbing Lichtenhahn Verlag, Elisabethenstrasse 8, 4051 Basel
Switzerland
www.helbing.ch

BarWrite® Press, PO Box 1308, Gracie Station, New York
United States
www.barwrite.com

Bibliographic information published by the Deutsche Nationalbibliothek
The Deutsche Nationalbibliothek lists this publication in the Deutsche
Nationalbibliografie; detailed bibliographic data are available in the
Internet at http://dnb.d-nb.de.

ISBN 978-3-9524737-0-2 (Lawbility)
ISBN 978-3-406-70828-2 (C.H.BECK)
ISBN 978-3-7190-3944-8 (Helbing Lichtenhahn)
ISBN-10: 0-9706088-8-8 (BarWrite®)
ISBN-13: 978-0-9706088-8-8 (BarWrite®)

eISBN 978-3-9524737-4-0 (ePub)*
eISBN 978-3-9524737-5-7 (mobi)*
* separate ISBN number for The Legal English Manual (e-book)

Graphic Design: Joel Dimitri Franz
Illustration: Anita Kurz

Preface

Proficiency in Legal English is a highly desirable skill. The Legal English Manual is the first of its kind to use a practice-oriented approach specifically geared to legal professionals who use Legal English in their practice. It is not a course book, but a handbook designed to provide practitioners with key legal terminology, along with explanations and examples of usage.

English has become the most global of languages, the lingua franca of international commerce, science, computing, and law. Even non-Anglo-American companies often choose English for international negotiations and agreements. For better or for worse, the use of English in international commerce and international law is inescapable. The ability to use Legal English competently and confidently has, thus, become a requirement for lawyers working in an international environment.

The Legal English Manual's authors are either practicing lawyers trained and licensed in the US, the UK, and civil law jurisdictions, or linguists with extensive experience teaching and coaching Legal English. The book also draws on the combined expertise of a wide network of coaches, legal practitioners, and linguists who work with Lawbility, a professional legal language and practical legal skills training institute based in Zurich, Switzerland.

Specifically designed for legal practitioners, the Legal English Manual is a practical reference book for legal professionals who want to "demonstrate their lawbility." We hope that it will provide you with the Legal English tools you need to take your legal practice to the next level.

Please send any comments you may have to legalenglish@lawbility.ch.

January 2017

Kathrin Weston Walsh
Editor

Jean-Luc Delli
Managing Director Lawbility Ltd.

Content

How to use this book

Introduction

This Manual is intended to help you expand your vocabulary and to improve your legal writing and speaking skills. It is not a legal text-book. Nor should you rely on the Manual as a source of legal advice. The Manual presents terminology and examples of usage in the context of Anglo-American law, as the language itself is conceptually bound to Anglo-American legal systems. Although the authors have made every effort to alert the reader to differences between the common law and the civil law context, you, as the reader, will have to exercise care when using legal terminology in different jurisdictions.

The book consists of three main sections:

I.   key legal terms relating to 14 areas of legal practice
II. practice manuals with templates for legal writing
III. practice manuals with templates for oral communication

Part I: Key legal terms relating to 14 areas of legal practice

Given space restrictions, the manual cannot cover every area of legal practice. Instead, it focuses on different aspects of commercial law.

Nevertheless, we have included criminal law and family law as well, in recognition of these fields' increasing importance in an international lawyer's practice.

Each separate manual in Part I follows the same pattern: first, principal content divided into sub-sections for easy reference; second, sample sentences; third, selected definitions; and fourth, the collocations corner.

The left-hand column of each sub-section sets out the principal legal terms you are likely to encounter in the context of each area of law. The accompanying text in the right-hand column then incorporates these terms in a typical legal context to help clarify each term's meaning.

A notation that a term is typical for the US or for the UK signifies that terms are used differently across jurisdictions, as follows:

• *plaintiff*	The *plaintiff* (UK: *claimant*) initiates legal proceedings; the *defendant* is the party against whom the plaintiff brings suit.
• *claimant*	
• *defendant*	

Following every sub-section, a sample sentence indicates how to use a selected term in practice, as follows:

Once a *complaint* has been *filed*, the court will *issue a summons* which is normally *served on* the *defendant*.

Each individual manual closes with the collocations corner. Collocations, or word partners, refer to words in English which naturally belong together. Collocations may be made up of

• a verb + a noun: *to incur costs*
• a verb + adverb: *to recommend strongly*
• or an adjective + noun: *a dramatic increase*

Legal English is rich in such word partnerships. Using them correctly helps to ensure that your Legal English is sophisticated and appropriately formal. In each collocations corner, we have tried to identify the word partners you are most likely to encounter in practice, as follows:

• *to instruct a lawyer*
• *to initiate legal proceedings*
• *to file a claim*
• *to lodge an appeal*
• *to bear the costs*

Part II: Practice manuals with templates for legal writing

These chapters set out authentic examples of the sort of correspondence and documents you may draft or receive in the course of your professional duties. The templates illustrate the layout and language of professional legal documents. **As with any legal drafting, the law may differ by jurisdiction, and there may be many different ways of expressing the same thing; hence, be aware that these templates are models only, and that you will have to customize all contracts and your correspondence for each transaction.**

The authors have also devoted particular attention to the differences between British English and American English. These differences occur not only in with regard to spelling – for example, defense counsel (US) and defence counsel (UK) – but also in date formats – 3/4/2016 (US) and 4.3.2016 (UK), or March 4, 2001 (US) and 3 April 2016 (UK); in the use of punctuation – Mr. Jones (US) and Mr Jones (UK); and even the choice of words or expressions when addressing the recipient of a letter or email – Dear Ms. Jones (US) or Dear Ms Jones (UK). You are, of course, free to adopt either American English or British English, but we recommend that correspondence and other documents be internally consistent.

Part III: Practice manuals with templates for oral communication

According to particular areas of practice or situations, the tables in Part III list useful terms and expressions you can memorize and use on the appropriate occasions. They will also help you to recognize – and appreciate – the language your colleagues, opposing counsel, and clients use. Again, be aware of what is appropriate in the context and culture in which you are operating.

In addition, this section includes helpful checklists to assist you in preparing for and conducting successful negotiations and client interviews.

Language notes

The abbreviations "US" and "UK" do not refer specifically to these countries themselves, but are intended to distinguish between the variations in legal terminology, spelling, or date formats in their respective regional variations of English.

Special feature

And, finally, the Legal English Manual leaves adequate space for you, the reader, to add your own comments and notes, as this is no coffee table book but a working manual!

I

Legal Terminology
Manuals for Practice Areas

1 Contract Law

A. Key Legal Terms

a. *Persons who have rights and obligations under a contract*

• *party*	A person who signs a contract is referred to
• *contracting party*	as a *party to* the contract, or a *contracting party*.
• *enter into*	Parties *enter into* a contract. In relation to each
• *counterparty*	other, each contracting party is the *counterparty*
• *perform*	to the other party. If a party does not *perform*
• *breaching party*	i.e. fulfill its obligations under the contract, it is
• *non-breaching/*	known as the *breaching party*. The counterparty is
injured party	the *non-breaching* (or *injured*) *party*. An interested
• *privity of contract*	person not in *privity of contract*, i.e., who is not
• *third party*	a contracting party, is known as a *third party*. A
• *third party*	third party who may benefit under a contract
beneficiary	is a *third party beneficiary*. A party who *assigns* its
• *assign*	rights and duties under a contract to another
• *assignor*	is the *assignor*; the recipient of those rights and
• *assignee*	obligations the *assignee*.

Under the terms of the contract, the *contracting parties* agreed to *perform* their respective obligations to their best endeavors.

b.   *Contract drafting*

- *draft*
- *draw up*
- *templates*
- *clauses*
- *sections*
- *provision*
- *paragraph*
- *whereas*
- *operative*
- *rights and obligations*
- *standard/ boilerplate clauses*
- *severability*
- *schedule*

Lawyers *draft* or *draw up* contracts, often with the help of contract models or *templates*. Contracts consist of *clauses* (or *sections*). Each clause contains a *provision*. If a clause consists of more than one *paragraph* it may be cited as, for example, clause 5, paragraph 2. Typically, a model commercial contract will commence with the names and addresses of the parties designated by a capitalized definition, e.g.: "This contract is entered into between Acme Ltd ("Seller") and Emca Holdings ("Purchaser")". This is generally followed by the *whereas* clause which is not an *operative* part of the contract but functions as a short introduction. The definitions section then lists the terms as they will be used in the contract. The agreement section sets out the parties' *rights and obligations*. *Standard clauses* (also known as *boilerplate* clauses) are generally found at the end of an agreement and may include provisions such as an applicable law clause or a *severability* clause (which provides that if for some reason a clause is unenforceable it may be severed or struck out without affecting the validity of the rest of the agreement). A *schedule* generally refers to very detailed agreements or information (such as a price list) put at the end of the contract for the sake of clarity; nevertheless, the content of the schedules remains part of the substantive agreement between the parties.

Now regarded as archaic, the introductory term *whereas* may be substituted by *Recitals* or *Background*, or even a statement such as: "This contract is made with reference to the following facts:"

c.   *Contract formation*

• *contract* • *agreement* • *binding* • *enforceable* • *formation/creation/ entering into* • *offer* • *acceptance* • *counter-offer* • *consideration*	A *contract* is an *agreement* that is *binding* and legally *enforceable*. A contract is *formed/created/entered into* when one party makes an *offer* which is then *accepted* by the other party. A *counter-offer* does not constitute acceptance. Under common law, for a contract to be properly formed and hence enforceable, legally sufficient *consideration* is also required. Often consideration is the purchase price, but it need not be money. It can be something else of value that induces the agreement.
• *signed* • *executed*	The parties may agree that the contract becomes binding when it has been *signed* (also *executed*) by both parties.
• *deed*	A *deed* is a special type of contract or binding commitment. The major difference between a deed and an agreement is that there is no requirement for consideration. Nevertheless, for the deed to be legally binding other conditions must be met, for example, the deed must be in writing, signed and witnessed, delivered, and clearly state that it is intended to be a deed.

In "the property was sold for $1 and other good and valuable *consideration*," the $1 is the tangible consideration (something real or concrete) which ensures that the contract is valid; the remaining amount is not revealed apart from the fact that it is "good," i.e. does not violate public policy, and is of value.

d.   *Contractual terms*

• *express* • *implied* • *oral* • *written* • *condition* • *warranty* • *guarantee* • *indemnity*	A contract may be *express* or *implied*, *oral* or *written*. A *condition* is a requirement which must be met for the contractual obligation(s) to be enforceable; a *warranty* is an assurance by one party that a statement of fact is true and may be relied upon by the other party; while a *guarantee* is a future promise e.g. to refund or repair defective goods. To *indemnify* is to compensate for, or cover the costs of, possible future loss.

The insurance company will *indemnify* the owner of the building against water damage.

e.   *Defenses to contract formation*

• *fraud* • *legal capacity* • *duress* • *undue influence* • *void* • *voidable* • *avoided*	A party may escape its obligations under a contract if it can prove, for example, *fraud*, lack of *legal capacity* (if one of the parties was a minor or insane), *duress* (being forced to enter into the agreement by the threat or use of force or other pressure), or *undue influence* (e.g. if a person was persuaded to sign a contract detrimental to that person's interests). Such contracts are not necessarily *void* or of no legal effect, but may be *voidable* (or *avoided* at the election of the minor or mentally incompetent person), which means the contract remains valid unless legitimately declared void.
• *illegality of the subject matter* • *void ab initio*	*Illegality of the subject matter* (e.g. a price-fixing agreement) renders a contract *void ab initio*, i.e. invalid from the beginning.

The contract was *voidable* because one of the parties was induced to enter into the contract by fraudulent means.

f.   *The end of the life of a contract*

* *expiration (US)/*
  expiry (UK)
* *termination*
* *cancellation*
* *rescission*
* *repudiation*
* *anticipatory breach*

In legal English there are a number of terms which indicate the end of the life of a contract. Some are synonyms, others have different meanings. *Expiration* is used when a contract has come to the end of its natural life as expressly set out in the contract itself. *Termination* typically refers to the ending of a contract. This may occur through the mutual consent of the parties even before the contract's anticipated *expiration* date. *Cancellation* puts an end to whatever remains to be performed under the contract, usually because the contract has been breached, or a party is in default. *Rescission* refers to the right of the parties to be returned to the status quo, i.e. to the position they were in before they entered into the contract. *Repudiation* (or *anticipatory breach*) refers to a party's refusal to perform under the contract.

Caveat: Although some of the terms above may be used interchangeably in some jurisdictions, other jurisdictions may attribute different meanings to the terms, which may then trigger different legal consequences.

This agreement is subject to *termination* at will by either party without notice.

Party A chose to *rescind* the contract following Party B's refusal to perform under the contract.

g. *Legal remedies*

• *remedy* • *damages* • *mitigation* • *liquidated damages* • *consequential damages/special damages*	If a party breaches a contract and the non-breaching party suffers a loss, the latter may file a claim for breach of contract and seek a *remedy* such as monetary compensation or *damages*. The non-breaching party has a duty to *mitigate* the loss, i.e. to limit the amount of *damage* the breach causes. *Liquidated damages* are a fixed sum agreed by the parties to be payable on a breach of contract by the breaching party to compensate the non-breaching party. *Consequential damages*, also known as special damages, are damages which do not arise directly from the breach but from the consequences of that breach.
• *material breach* • *award* • *equitable remedy* • *specific performance* • *injunction*	If the breach was *material*, the contract may be terminated. If the plaintiff prevails in an action against the defendant for breach of contract, the court may *award* damages, or, under special circumstances, order non-monetary *equitable remedies* (UK/US) such as *specific performance* (whereby the defendant is ordered to fulfill his or her obligations under the contract), or issue an *injunction*, i.e. order a party to do or refrain from doing a particular act. Note that in the US, the Uniform Commercial Code (UCC), which applies to contracts for the sale of goods, employs different terminology in some circumstances.

The contract provided for *liquidated damages* in the amount of $2,500 for each day that construction of the bridge was delayed.

B.   Sample Definitions

consideration	Common law concept in connection with contracts: what is done in return for the promise or act of another party in order for a contract to be properly performed or enforceable.
indemnity	Obligation to compensate someone, or the compensation provided to someone for loss, damage, or expense.
voidable	A contract is voidable if it appears to be enforceable but in fact suffers from some defect that entitles one or both parties to rescind the contract or have it declared unenforceable by a court.

C.   Collocations Corner

a.   Clause(s)

→ **to amend a clause**

to change a clause, usually slightly, or to cause the characteristics of a clause to change (syn.: to modify)	Amending a clause in the contract could mean delaying the entire transaction.

→ **to construe a clause**

to understand the meaning, especially of a contract clause, in a particular way to interpret a document, word, or an act in a certain way	As each party construed the best efforts clause to mean something different, the court found the clause to be ambiguous.

→ to draft a clause

to prepare something, usually an official document, in writing (syn.: to draw up) to outline the initial/ preliminary version of a document, including the main points but not necessarily all the details	The associates were asked to draft a clause that would grant their firm full protection.

→ to interpret a clause

to determine the intended meaning of something to understand the meaning of a clause/contract in a particular way	As the contract was originally in Spanish, it was hard to determine whether the English-speaking parties had interpreted the clause correctly.

→ to modify a clause

to change a clause, usually slightly, or to cause the characteristics of a clause to change (syn.: to amend)	The clause may need to be modified to include past as well as present income.

→ to negotiate a clause

to try to reach an agreement with someone by formally discussing the subject matter	The client was no longer willing to negotiate the compensation clause.

→ to refer to a clause

to mention/relate (to) a person, thing, or concept	Section II of the contract referred to numerous clauses in Section I of the contract.

› to strike (out) a clause

to delete, eliminate, or remove a word, sentence, or paragraph	The parties decided to strike (out) the entire clause.

b.   Contract

→ to amend a contract

to make changes to a sentence, document, or situation	After almost thirty years, we had to amend the contract.

→ to avoid a contract

to relieve all the parties to a contract from their duties, because it has been legally recognized that it is inequitable or impossible to continue performance	The following section sets out all the circumstances in which the contract may be avoided.

→ to be bound by a contract

to have a legal obligation to do something	Section 2.1 specifically outlines all the products your client is bound by contract to deliver.

→ to breach a contract

to fail to fulfill/perform the duties set out by a contract to break the legal obligations set out by a contract	Failing to pay the stated amount of money would mean breaching the contract.

→ to construe a contract

to understand the meaning, especially of a contract clause, in a particular way to interpret a document, word, or an act in a certain way	The judge construed the contract in a commercially equitable manner.

→ to draft a contract

to prepare something, usually an official document, in writing (syn.: to draw up) to outline the initial/ preliminary version of a document, including the main points but not necessarily all the details	If you are unsure of how to draft a contract, I would recommend reviewing the standard form contracts first.

→ to draw up a contract

to prepare something, usually an official document, in writing	Becky was unsure about the contract she had drawn up, so she gave it to her partner to review.

→ to enforce a contract

to compel someone to act in accordance with the rule/law/contract	As they failed to comply with their contractual obligations on several occasions, I had no choice but to ask the court to enforce the contract.

→ to enter into a contract

to formally, legally agree to a contract with another party	After months of negotiating, Company A entered into an agreement with Company B.

→ to execute a contract

to sign a contract	The draft of the contract is now ready for the parties to execute.

→ to honor a contract

to fulfill the terms of a contract to act in accordance with the demands of the contract	To honor this contract, you must provide the remainder of the goods by Monday.

→ **to interpret a contract**

to determine the intended meaning of something	Scholars have written entire books on how to interpret contracts.
to understand the meaning of a text/clause/contract in a particular way	

→ **to modify a contract**

to change a contract, usually slightly, or to cause the characteristics of a clause to change (syn.: to amend)	At the client's request, the lawyer modified the contract to reflect that the client would be an employee rather than an independent contractor.

→ **to negotiate a contract**

to try to reach an agreement with someone by formally discussing the subject matter	After months of negotiating, we finally reached an agreement.

→ **to perform a contract**

to act in accordance with (to fulfill) the duties under a contract	He knew that if he did not perform the contract, he might face litigation.

→ **to refer to a contract**

to mention/to relate (to) a contract	If you are unsure about your obligations that arise with this partnership, it would help to refer to the contract you signed a month ago.

→ **to repudiate a contract**

to refuse to carry out the obligations under a contract	As the conditions of his employment had changed substantially, he chose to repudiate his employment contract.

→ to rescind a contract

to annul a contract, thereby taking away its legal power and returning all parties to the positions they were in before entering into the contract, usually on the basis of fraud or significant mutual mistake	If the parties have legitimate grounds for rescinding a contract, a court will, in many cases, deem the contract never to have existed, and will issue an order that the parties be returned to the status quo existing before they entered into the contract.

→ to set aside a contract

the decision made by the court to terminate the contract, thereby deeming the contract avoided	Setting aside the contract was the best possible outcome.

→ to terminate a contract

to bring something (a contract) to an end; it will therefore cease to have any legal power	During this presentation, I will outline the circumstances in which the parties can terminate a contract.

→ to treat a contract as binding upon

to determine that a contract creates legally enforceable rights and duties for the parties to comply with its terms and conditions a binding agreement creates duties that should not be breached	The courts recognized that the contract was signed under duress, and therefore did not treat it as binding upon the parties.

c.   *Contractual rights*

→ to confer contractual rights

to grant/extend a contractual right to someone	Mr. Clark's actions seem to have exceeded the rights the contract conferred upon him.

→ to enforce contractual rights

to compel someone to act in accordance with the rule/law/contract	The rule clearly states that third parties to a contract can also sue to enforce their contractual rights.

→ to exercise contractual rights

to apply and use one's rights under a contract	The lawyer advised his client to exercise his contractual right to terminate the contract.

→ to forfeit contractual rights

to lose or surrender a contractual right as a result of wrongdoing	After the Board discovered that the Chairman had embezzled funds, he forfeited most of the contractual rights his employment agreement had granted him.

→ to grant contractual rights

to give certain contractual rights to someone in a legal or formal context	The contract granted them the right to utilize the apartment in whichever manner they pleased.

→ to sign away contractual rights

to renounce or give away rights (syn.: to waive)	In return for a substantial payment, the former employee signed away any right to sue the company on claims related to his employment agreement.

→ to transfer contractual rights

to award/sell/hand over your rights to someone else	The lawyers were discussing whether it was possible to transfer her contractual rights to a non-party to the agreement.

→ to waive contractual rights

to give up a right or refrain from demanding a right (syn.: to sign away)	The company waived its right to enforce the non-competition agreement after the former employee agreed to return his entire signing bonus.

d.   *Damages*

→ to award damages	
to compel one party to compensate the other for the injury suffered or for the loss that was caused	The court found that Don had breached his contract with Sue and awarded her damages in the amount of $200,000.

→ to claim damages	
to request/demand compensation from another party	The plaintiff claimed damages of $600,000 relating to the defendant's breach of the contract.

→ to demand damages	
to request something in a forceful manner to insist upon something	I demand one million dollars in damages.

→ to mitigate damages	
to take measures to make damages or other negative consequences resulting from a breach less severe	The injured party has a duty to mitigate its damages.

→ to pay damages	
to give money/to bear a cost to compensate	The plaintiff has asked that the defendant pay damages in full immediately, rather than in installments.

→ to recover damages	
to obtain/get/receive damages (compensation) pursuant to a court ruling	The plaintiff cannot recover damages unless he can prove that the defendant's breach of contract actually resulted in economic harm.

→ to seek damages	
to ask for/request damages from the court	They sought damages after he breached the contract's confidentiality clause.

1

→ to stipulate to damages

to come to an agreement about the sum of damages to be paid, should a breach of contract occur, to minimize the scope of the dispute that would have to be settled by the court	In the liquidated damages clause, the parties stipulated to the precise amount of damages should a contractual breach occur.

→ to waive damages

to give up a right or refrain from demanding a right (syn.: to sign away)	After careful consideration, the plaintiff decided to waive his contractual right to seek damages, as he knew a lawsuit would cause the defendent to go bankrupt.

→ to win damages

to succeed in obtaining damages	As the evidence was too weak, the plaintiff did not win any damages.

e.   Obligations

→ to carry out obligations

to do something in order to fulfill your obligations (syn.: to perform, to fulfill, to meet)	The only reason they still attend the staff meetings is to carry out the obligations set out in their employment contract.

→ to comply with obligations

to act in accordance with the obligations set out in the contract to obey the contract's terms and conditions	It is crucial for both companies to comply with the obligations set out by the partnership agreement.

→ to discharge from obligations

to release/relieve someone of his obligations	After terminating the contract, he was discharged from any further obligations to his business partner.

→ to fulfill (US)/fulfil (UK) obligations

to execute/perform a required act (syn.: to carry out, to perform, to meet)	Fulfilling the obligations set out by the contract should be your first priority.

→ to impose obligations

to create or place an obligation on someone	The separation agreement may impose an obligation on the higher-earning spouse to pay child support following a divorce.

→ to meet obligations

to fulfill one's responsibilities (syn.: to carry out, to perform)	You are under a contractual duty to meet the obligations set out in the first clause.

→ to perform obligations

to act in accordance with the duties under a contract (syn.: to carry out, to fulfill, to meet)	Absent a good legal reason not to do so, the parties must perform all of their contractual obligations.

f.   *Offer*

→ to accept an offer

to agree to the conditions of the offer to say yes to an offer	He was eager to accept the offer, as he thought it would greatly benefit his career.

→ to decline an offer

to refuse (syn.: to reject, to turn down)	Given its unfavorable pricing terms, he declined the seller's initial offer.

→ to extend an offer

to propose/present an offer (syn.: to make)	She extended an offer to them to purchase a license for the new technology she had developed.

→ to make an offer

to propose/present an offer (syn.: to extend)	His resume was so impressive that we made him an offer immediately after the interview.

→ **to refuse an offer**

to decline (syn.: to reject, to turn down) to state that you will not accept an offer	Your offer was very generous indeed, but unfortunately I will have to refuse it for personal reasons.

→ **to reject an offer**

to decline (syn.: to refuse, to turn down)	As the outlined conditions are unacceptable, I have no choice but to reject your offer.

→ **to revoke an offer**

to officially declare that an offer is no longer legally valid to annul by rescinding the offer	The human resources manager wants to know whether he can still revoke the offer without any negative legal consequences.

→ **to turn down an offer**

to decline (syn.: to refuse, to reject)	We were surprised when he turned down our employment offer.

→ **to withdraw an offer**

to take back/discontinue an offer	After finding out about his hidden criminal record, she decided to withdraw the offer.

g. *Performance*

→ **to render performance**

to carry out in accordance with the terms and conditions outlined by a contract	Should you fail to render performance by the end of the week, I will sue you for breach of contract.

h.   *Miscellaneous*

→ to assign a contractual right

to attribute/hand over/ sell/transfer certain contractual rights to someone else	Should you ever be unable to perform, you can assign your contractual rights to your son, giving him all the benefits that arise under the contract.

→ to be liable for

to be responsible for something or someone under the law	Unfortunately, taking all the facts into consideration, I have to inform you that you are indeed liable for breaching the contract.

→ to confer a benefit on

to grant/extend a benefit	Your Honor, the sole purpose of this clause is to confer a benefit on my client.

→ to incur costs

to be liable/responsible for costs	We seek to recover the substantial costs our client incurred because your client breached the contract.

→ to reach an agreement

to arrive at an agreement to come to an agreement	I have no desire to extend these negotiations any further, so we have to reach an agreement today.

→ to rely on an agreement

to depend on an agreement previously made	It was irresponsible of my daughter to rely on their verbal agreement without requesting a contract in writing.

→ to set out/stipulate the terms and conditions

to demand/indicate expressly what the terms and conditions of an agreement should be	They did not stipulate the terms and conditions, and only requested that I financially support their endeavors.

→ to suffer damages/injury/loss

to experience economic loss	The damages my client suffered as a result of your client's failure to deliver the goods on time include paying a substantially higher price for replacement goods.

2   Tort Law

A.   Key Legal Terms

a.   General

• *tort* • *civil wrong* • *damages* • *breach of contract*	A *tort*, in common law jurisdictions, is a non-contractual *civil wrong* which constitutes a wrongful act or omission for which *damages* can be obtained in a civil court by the person who has been harmed. Tort law may provide remedies that are separate from and in addition to remedies for *breach of contract* and penalties for criminal actions.
• *personal injury* • *property damage* • *remedy* • *injunction* • *tortfeasor* • *joint tortfeasors*	Tort law is mainly concerned with providing compensation for *personal injury* and *property damage.* The main *remedy* for a tort is an action for damages, although in certain cases an *injunction* can be obtained to prevent a repetition of the tort. The *tortfeasor* is the one who commits a tort, and there can be *joint tortfeasors*.
• *delict*	The equivalent of a tort in civil law jurisdictions is technically called a delict. The concept of a delict typically covers intentional, willful, or negligent acts which give rise to a legal obligation between parties even though the parties have not entered into a contract. While lawyers in some jurisdictions may use the term "tort" as a non-technical term to refer to a non-contractual delict or other wrongful act which one party perpetrates upon another, the civil law concept of a delict differs in many substantive ways from the common law tort concept.

A taxi driver who causes injury by negligent driving may be liable in tort for personal injury caused.

b.   *Types of torts*

• *causation*	The four essential elements of a negligence claim under common law are (i) duty of one party toward another, (ii) breach of that duty by an act or omission, (iii) *causation* (in that a party's breach of its duty actually causes harm to another), and (iv) damages to another party. However, common law jurisdictions also recognize numerous specific causes of action in tort, for which additional elements (set forth in the case law) must be met.
• *defamation* • *slander* • *libel* • *assault* • *false imprisonment* • *trespass* • *nuisance* • *tortious*	In common law jurisdictions, in addition to providing compensation for personal injury, tort law also protects other interests such as a person's reputation (i.e. *defamation* – which can take the form of either *slander* [oral] or *libel* [published]) and a person's personal freedom from *assault* or *false imprisonment*. Real property is protected from *trespass*, and enjoyment of property can be protected from *nuisance* caused by noise or pollution.
• *economic torts* • *negligent misrepresentation*	*Economic torts* are intended to protect businesses from interference with their trade, so, for example, a victim of *negligent misrepresentation* may recover damages for financial loss caused by detrimental reliance on the tortfeasor's statement.

• *negligence*	Torts can be *negligent* (e.g. failure to keep a publicly accessible walkway for which one is responsible clear of ice and snow) or intentional (e.g. *fraud*).
• *fraud*	
• *strict liability*	
• *animals*	
• *dangerous items*	The law also recognizes some *strict liability* torts, for which the plaintiff need not prove that the defendant breached a duty. Examples of strict liability torts may include those involving certain *animals*, particularly *dangerous items*, and *product liability* claims.
• *product liability*	

In the interests of consumer protection, a *product liability* directive was introduced by the European Union requiring manufacturers to pay for any damage resulting from defective products.

Personal Notes _____

_____

_____

_____

_____

_____

_____

_____

_____

c.   *Vicarious liability*

• *vicarious liability*
• *vicariously liable*
• *ratified*

Vicarious liability is a doctrine of common law tort/agency law. Legal liability can, thus, also be imposed on one person for torts committed by another person even though the defendant is not personally at fault. Employers, for example, may be *vicariously liable* for an employee's torts when they have authorized or *ratified* the activity or when the tort is committed within the authorized scope of an employee's work.

• *to pursue legal action*

One purpose of vicarious liability is to ensure that employers pay the costs of the damage caused by their business operations. The employer's liability is in addition to that of the employee, who may still be personally liable for his or her own tort. The person harmed by the tort may sue either or both the employer and employee, but may prefer to *pursue legal action* against the employer.

A supermarket employee spills paint on a customer. Legal action may be taken against either the employee or the employer, but may be more practical against the latter for economic reasons. The employee's action has harmed the plaintiff, but his employer may bear vicarious liability for the harm.

d.   Causation and duty of care

• *proximate cause* • *intervening cause* • *extent*	The plaintiff must prove that the harm was actually caused by the tort that he or she is suing for (US/UK: *proximate cause*); the defendant may argue that there was a superseding *intervening cause*. It is also necessary to show that legally recognized harm was directly or indirectly caused by the tortfeasor, in addition to which the plaintiff must prove the *extent* of the damage.
• *duty of care* • *burden of proof* • *dereliction*	Negligence is a breach of a legal *duty of care* resulting in damage to the plaintiff. The *burden of proof* falls on the plaintiff who, in common law systems, must show that he or she was owed a duty and that there was a *dereliction* or breach of that duty.
• *damages* • *harm* • *remote*	It must then be established that the tortfeasor (or, in some cases, his or her employee or agent) caused the injury or harm and that the plaintiff suffered *damages* as a result of that breach. Finally, it must be shown that the harm was not too *remote* – in other words that proximate cause existed.

When a plaintiff alleges that a defendant's actions caused the plaintiff's injury, but puts forward no evidence linking the defendant's actions to the injury, the plaintiff cannot meet his burden of proof.

2

e.   Defenses

• *absolve*	A successful defense can *absolve* the defendant from liability for the tort claim which the plaintiff has brought. A successful defense can lie, for example, in a showing that the defendant owed no duty to the plaintiff, that the defendant did not breach any duty to the plaintiff, that any breach by the defendant was not the cause of the harm to the plaintiff, or that the defendant's breach of a duty to the plaintiff did not result in any damages to the plaintiff.
• *contributory negligence* • *illegality* • *consent* • *"volenti non fit iniuria"* • *mitigation defense* • *comparative negligence* • *"ex turpi causa non oritur actio"*	These defenses may also include *contributory negligence* and *illegality* (US/UK) or *consent*. Typically, the plaintiff cannot hold another liable in tort for actions to which the plaintiff has consented (Latin: *volenti non fit iniuria*). Pursuant to the common law *mitigation defense* of contributory negligence, a plaintiff was totally barred from recovery if the plaintiff himself or herself was negligent in causing the accident. Many jurisdictions have now abolished the doctrine of contributory negligence in favor of a *comparative negligence* defense. Under a comparative negligence approach, a judge or jury will allocate damages in cases when both the plaintiff and the defendant were negligent to some degree. In some jurisdictions, illegality may disallow a tort action if the claimant is involved in wrongdoing or criminal behavior at the time the alleged negligence occurred; this may extinguish or reduce the defendant's liability (Latin: *ex turpi causa non oritur actio*).

A person who is injured while participating in a boxing match may not have a cause of action in tort on the grounds of *volenti non fit iniuria*.

f. *Limitation of liability*

• *statutory rules* • *statute of limitations* • *time-barred*	*Statutory rules* limit the time within which civil actions such as tort can be brought against the tortfeasor. The expiration of a *statute of limitations* may provide a defendant with a complete defense to a claim in tort; hence, unless the claim is filed with the appropriate judicial authority within the stipulated period from the date of the tort, the claim will most likely be *time-barred*.
• *cause of action*	Different tort *causes of action* can have different statutes of limitations, meaning that the *limitation period* within which a plaintiff can bring a cause of action for damages differs depending on the nature of the tort at issue.

B. Sample Definitions

causation/causal connection	Link between the defendant's intentional or negligent act and the loss or damages suffered by the plaintiff.
negligence	Failure to exercise a particular duty of care.
statute of limitations	Period of time within which a claim must be filed.

C.   Collocations Corner

→ to absolve from liability

to declare free from guilt/ responsibility/punishment	The judge found that the defendant had met the required standard of care and was, therefore, absolved from liability for the damages resulting to the plaintiff's property.

→ to accrue a right of action (UK only)

to obtain the right to initiate a claim against someone at the time the event that caused the damages, loss, or harm is deemed to have occurred	She accrued a right of action against her teacher last Tuesday when the accident occurred.

→ to affirm a decision/ruling/judgment

to uphold a lower court's decision	The Supreme Court affirmed the Appeals Court's decision on all points.

→ to allege negligence

to claim that someone has failed to exercise the required standard of care, resulting in injury, loss, or damages	Harry's lawyer alleges that the driver's negligence caused Harry's injury.

→ to allocate liability

to determine to what extent different parties are liable for a harm or loss	While it was evident that the manufacturer, the distributor, and the seller of chemicals were all responsible for contaminating the water, the court struggled with allocating liability for the contamination among the three parties.

→ to appeal a decision/ruling/judgment

to request review of a decision by a higher court	The lawyer appealed the District Court's decision.

→ to attribute blame

to regard a certain act as having been caused by something/someone	The judge attributed the blame for the accident to Mr. Jones.

2

→ to award costs

to grant the successful party in legal proceedings the right to receive payment from the losing party to cover certain legal expenses (usually distinct from attorney's fees), such as travel, deposition, or exhibit costs	The court awarded costs to Mr. Hall in the amount of $85,000.

→ to award damages

to compel one party to compensate the other for the injury suffered or for the loss that was caused	The court awarded the woman who was hit by a bicycle on the sidewalk damages in the amount of $200,000.

→ to be liable for

to be legally responsible for something	The plaintiff claimed that the building's owner should be liable for the ice outside the building that caused the plaintiff to slip and fall.

→ to bear responsibility

to be personally responsible or liable for something/ someone	Writing a visa invitation letter for her may mean that you bear legal responsibility in case she decides to overstay her visa.

→ to breach a duty

to fail to fulfill/perform one's legal obligations to others to adhere to a reasonable standard of care.	The employer breached his duty of care, as he did not take the required actions to ensure the health and well-being of his employee.

→ to cause harm/damages

to damage, injure, or hurt and thereby bring about pain or suffering	The harm he caused was not so serious as to amount to grievous bodily harm. (Under UK law, this is serious injury.)

→ to cause injury

| to engage in an act that brought about pain, damages, or loss to someone else, for which the law provides remedies | The defendant caused injury to my client, resulting in high hospital fees as well as pain and suffering. |

→ to claim/seek damages

| to request/demand compensation from another party | The plaintiff claimed/sought damages of $600,000 as compensation for his injuries. |

→ to commit a tort

| to carry out a wrongful act or infringement of a right, other than a contractual right, whether intentionally or negligently, which leads to civil legal liability | Hank committed the tort of trespassing on private property. |

→ to demand compensation

| to request payment in a forceful manner to insist upon payment | I demand compensation in the amount of $1,000,000. |

→ to deny allegations

| to deny claims of liability for committing an offense | He denied all allegations against him. |

→ to dismiss a case

| to terminate, by court decision, court proceedings, prior to trial or prior to rendering a judgment Note: a dismissal with prejudice is permanent, while a case dismissed without prejudice can be refiled after the parties cure the defects underlying the dismissal without prejudice | The judge dismissed the case with prejudice on the grounds that the applicable statute of limitations had run. |

2

→ to engage in tortious conduct

| to carry out an illegal and improper act, whether intentionally or negligently, which leads to civil legal liability | By assaulting his employee, George engaged in tortious conduct. |

→ to enter/raise a defense

| to put forth arguments and reasoning against a claim in an attempt to avoid liability | The defendant raised the defense of failure to mitigate in an attempt to reduce his exposure to liability. |

→ to establish negligence

| to prove that the elements of negligence occurred (i.e. existence of a duty, breach of that duty, causation, and damages) | The lawyer was able to establish negligence after proving all the elements of negligence in court. |

→ to hold liable

| to deem someone responsible for something under the law | We understand that the court will hold the company liable for polluting the water. |

→ to incur costs

| to be liable/responsible for costs | We seek to recover the substantial costs our client incurred in pursuing this legal action. |

→ to incur loss/damages

| to incur physical, emotional, economic, or other harm or loss (syn.: to suffer damages) | After a former employee revealed highly confidential trade secrets to a competitor, the company incurred significant economic damages. |

→ to meet the standard of care

| to comply with the appropriate level of care set by law for a particular action | Employees who operate heavy machinery generally have to meet a certain standard of care in performing their duties. |

→ to mitigate damages/harm

to take steps to reduce damages or injury following an action that causes harm	After they realized that a portion of the canned goods they produced had been contaminated by bacteria, they attempted to mitigate any damages by immediately recalling all the goods they had produced during the relevant time period.

→ to owe a duty

to have a legal obligation to others to adhere to a reasonable standard of care	The employer owed his employee a duty of care to ensure his health and well-being.

→ to pay damages

to give money/ to compensate for losses	The plaintiff has asked that the defendant pay damages in full immediately, rather than in installments.

→ to prove damages/harm

to establish that the plaintiff suffered physical, financial, emotional, or other loss or injury	While the lawyer proved that the plaintiff suffered harm, the defense questioned whether or not the defendant's act had caused the harm.

→ to prove fault

to demonstrate that someone negligently or intentionally acted in contravention of the law, causing injury or damages to another	The lawyer does not have to prove fault, because the defendant admitted liability.

→ to provide compensation

to award a remedy to someone who has suffered harm/injury as compensation for the losses incurred	My lawyer suggested in discussing settlement options that we ask my employer to provide monetary compensation to avoid taking this case to trial.

→ to recover damages

to obtain/get/receive damages (compensation) pursuant to a court ruling	The plaintiff cannot recover damages unless he can prove that the defendant's act caused the plaintiff's injury.

→ to reverse a decision/ruling/judgment

to set aside or change a prior court decision	The Court of Appeals reversed the District Court's ruling against Harry.

→ to rule in favor of a party/find for a party

to support and uphold a party's claims and thereby find against the opposing party	The judge ruled in Dale's favor on the question of damages.

→ to rule on a case

to evaluate a case and reach a decision	The judge ruled on the case between John and Mary.

→ to seek damages

to ask for/request damages from the court	His parents sought damages from the hospital that treated him for the wrong disease.

→ to settle an action/claim/lawsuit

to resolve a legal matter between disputing parties extrajudicially either before or after court action begins	The two parties agreed to settle the action before the matter went to trial.

→ to sue in tort/to bring an action in tort

to institute legal proceedings against someone for carrying out a wrongful act or infringement of a non-contractual right, leading to civil legal liability	Harry sued in tort for the injury he had suffered.

→ to suffer damages/injury/loss

to incur physical, emotional, economic, or other harm or loss (syn.: to incur damages)	The complaint states that the plaintiff suffered damages in the amount of $750,000 as a result of the defendant's actions.

→ to sustain injury

to incur (usually physical) harm or suffering	He is unable to work because of the injuries he sustained during his car accident.

→ to take/initiate/conduct a claim/action/lawsuit

to commence legal action by filing a complaint	He initiated a negligence case against his former doctor.

→ to waive a right

to give up a right or refrain from demanding a right (syn.: to sign away)	After careful consideration, the plaintiff decided to waive his right to seek damages, because he knew it would cause the defendant to go bankrupt.

→ to win/be entitled to damages

to succeed in obtaining damages	As the evidence was too weak, the plaintiff did not win any damages.

Personal Notes _____

_____

_____

_____

_____

_____

_____

_____

3

3 Company/Corporate Law

A. Key Legal Terms

a. *Characteristics*

• *corporation* • *company* • *private* • *shareholding* • *public* • *stock*	A *corporation* or a *company* is a legal entity registered with the appropriate corporate register. It can be either a *private* company where the *shareholding* is held by a restricted group, or a *public* company with its *stock* quoted on the stock exchange and freely traded. As a result, shares or stock (US) in public companies can be bought by members of the public. A share is a unit that represents the holder's interest in a company.
• *limited liability company* • *membership interest*	In the US, a *limited liability company (LLC)* is a legal entity that combines elements of partnership and corporate structures. A member of an LLC possesses a *membership interest*.
• *limited liability* • *separate legal personality* • *perpetual succession* • *pierce the corporate veil*	Both types of legal entity (corporation and LLC) may have *limited liability*, hence providing the owners with protection if the entity becomes insolvent. Both the corporation and the LLC also have a *separate legal personality*, meaning that they can sue or be sued, and enjoy *perpetual succession*, allowing the entities to survive their members.

In some jurisdictions, a single shareholder or member may establish both the corporation and the LLC. A court may *pierce the corporate veil* to disregard the entity's separate legal personality where the fiction of a separate legal personality is abused, e.g. where there is sufficient evidence of fraudulent conduct.

b.   Members

• *ordinary shares* • *equity capital* • *registered shares* • *bearer shares* • *preference shares* • *dividend* • *authorized share capital* • *memorandum of association* • *articles of association* • *bylaws* • *issued share capital*	*Ordinary shares* represent the risk capital or *equity capital* in the corporation. They may be *registered shares* (which are made out to the owner) or *bearer shares* (where the holder of the share in the corporation is unknown). *Preference shares* confer certain privileges with regard to the shareholder's proprietary rights. In some jurisdictions, a company will not be restricted to any maximum amount of shares it can issue, previously referred to as *authorized share capital* in the *memorandum* and *articles of association* (US: Certificate of Incorporation and *bylaws* respectively). *The issued share capital* refers to the shares actually held by the shareholders.
• *Annual General Meeting* • *board of directors* • *auditors* • *company secretary*	The shareholders of the corporation are required by law to meet once a year by way of an *Annual General Meeting* (AGM), for example to elect the *board of directors* and appoint the *auditors*. In the US and UK every public company is required to have a *company secretary* (US: *secretary*) who is responsible for the administrative and filing duties imposed on the company by the relevant corporate legislation.

The board's proposal to increase the *equity capital* of the corporation by issuing new shares was refused by the shareholders.

c.   *Organization*

• *extraordinary shareholders' meetings* • *notice period* • *agenda* • *shareholders' resolutions*	The AGM will, in general, be called by the board of directors. *Extraordinary shareholders' meetings* can be called as often as the board of directors deems necessary. When calling a shareholders' meeting the board of directors must observe a *notice period*, and an *agenda* must be provided to the shareholders. Finally, a shareholders' meeting may be convened at any time if all shareholders are present. Decisions reached at shareholders' meetings are called *shareholders' resolutions*. In general, shareholders' resolutions are reached by a simple majority, assuming a quorum is present. Some important decisions may only be reached by a qualified majority.
• *bylaws/ articles of association* • *quorum* • *board resolutions* • *minutes* • *ratified*	The board of directors is the highest authority for the administration and management of a corporation. The board meets in accordance with the corporation's *bylaws* (UK: *articles of association*) and, providing that such meetings have the necessary *quorum*, can conduct most day to day company business by way of *board resolutions* recorded in the company's *minutes*. Because the shareholders are the owners of the company, some board resolutions may need to be *ratified* by them.

The board of directors *resolved to proceed* with negotiations to acquire XYZ after a resolution to this effect was *ratified* by the shareholders

B.   Sample Definitions

corporation	A corporation is a legal entity with legal capacity formed in accordance with the relevant legislation, registered with the appropriate corporate register and owned and controlled by its members, who may be natural persons or legal entities themselves.
membership interest	Share of the registered capital of a company held by an individual member.
bylaws	The bylaws (US), or articles of association (UK) are the constitution of a corporate body such as a corporation, which set out the rights and obligations of its members and management bodies.

Personal Notes _____

_____

_____

_____

_____

_____

_____

C.   Collocations Corner

→ to be liable for a company debt

to be legally responsible and accountable for a company's borrowed money	Alex is personally liable for the company's debt of $500,000.
Tip: creditors may pursue the liable person's home, bank account, investments and other assets to satisfy the corporate debt	

→ to call/convene a meeting

to request that people assemble in order to discuss company matters	Bill suggested we call a meeting to further discuss the funding of his project.
Tip: there may be specific requirements for calling meetings under the company constitution or law	

→ to conduct company business

to carry out or execute company-related matters	They had to travel to Germany to conduct company business with their most important clients.
to carry on business operations	

→ to confer a privilege

to grant or extend a right that is solely given to one person or a class of people	The company confers important privileges upon its majority shareholders.

→ to distribute dividends

to distribute a portion of corporate profits to shareholders	The corporation distributed a dividend of $0.55 per share.

3

→ to draft/draw up Articles of Association/ Articles of Incorporation

to prepare an official document containing the purpose of the company and stating the duties and responsibilities of its members	The lawyer drafted the Articles of Incorporation for the new entity.
Tip: the Articles of Association/Incorporation are necessary to register a company	

→ to elect the board of directors

to vote, as a shareholder in a general meeting, on the appointment of company directors	The shareholders elected five new members to the board of directors at today's general meeting.

→ to exercise/enforce rights as a shareholder

to use or apply certain legal shareholder rights (i.e. voting power, transferral of ownership)	Jacob exercised his right as a shareholder to vote on the merger of the company.

→ to file for bankruptcy/to file for protection/ to open bankruptcy proceedings

to initiate a court action for relief from debts by making court-approved plans for partial repayment	The ABC Trading Company filed for bankruptcy after it became unable to service its debts.

→ to have/hold rights in the management of a business/ company

to possess certain legal rights and discretion in managing a company, i.e. core rights (relating to budgets, strategy etc.) and operational rights (hiring, termination, other personnel decisions)	Fred held rights in the management of Greenies Ltd.

→ to hold shares

to have shares in a company	The investor bought shares and held them for ten years.

→ to increase the share capital

to increase a company's capital by issuing new shares or by transferring company equity toward share capital	Increasing his company's share capital was a bold but irresponsible move.

→ to issue shares

to sell existing shares or offer new shares on the market, or to put new shares on the market for sale to the public	The company's shareholders had no choice but to issue shares on the market to repay the company's debts.

→ to limit member's/shareholders liability

to cap shareholders' liability for company debts and obligations to the par value of his or her fully paid shares	Members of Austra LLC knew they would benefit from limited liability.

→ to manage the affairs of a company in compliance with the law

to be responsible for the company's internal and external communications in line with rules and regulations, including public relations, employee attitudes, and government relations	Tim failed to manage the affairs of Blue & Co. in compliance with the law.

→ to offer quoted stock

to offer shares that can be purchased or sold on a stock market, whereby information about the stock (such as bid, last trading price) is stated (quoted)	Information regarding the quoted stock a company offers is usually available online.

→ to owe fiduciary duties

to have the legal obligation, as a director, to act in the company's best interests, including by avoiding conflicts of interest and by discharging one's duties as a director with an appropriate level of skill	As a director of the company, Bianca owed fiduciary duties to the corporation.

→ to pass a shareholders' resolution

to reach a decisions at a shareholders' meeting, which generally requires a majority or a qualified majority vote	Frank, a shareholder of the second biggest oil firm in Nebraska, needed at least ten votes from other shareholders to pass the proposed shareholders' resolution.

→ to pay debts and liabilities of a company

to pay back money that a corporate entity previously borrowed from a creditor	The company paid a debt of $2,000,000 to the bank.

→ to pierce/lift the corporate veil

to disregard an entity's separate corporate identity to hold its shareholders, directors, or officers personally liable for the actions or debts of a company	A court may pierce the corporate veil if it has evidence that a company's corporate form serves the purpose of evading a presently existing legal obligation, or if the evidence demonstrates an insufficiently clear legal separation between the assets and decisions of the corporate entity and those of its officers and directors.

→ to possess/own an interest in a company

to have a portion of shares in a company, which can be controlling (greater than 50%) or non-controlling (less than 50%)	Michelle owned a controlling interest of 80% in Bent Ltd.

→ to proceed with negotiations

to continue with discussions in order to come to a final agreement	The sudden changes in the economy might have caused some minor setbacks, but I am willing to proceed with negotiations as soon as possible.

→ to ratify a board resolution

to vote upon, validate, and put into force a board resolution, which is a written document outlining the decisions of a company's board of directors during a meeting	The directors had all agreed to ratify the board resolution from the meeting held in January.

→ to require by law

to determine that something is mandatory by law	After Freddy did some research, he compiled a document outlining which employee benefits the company was required by law to provide.

→ to resolve to proceed

to make the formal decision to continue something as previously planned	Although the parties were unable to reach a mutual agreement on the compensation aspects of the employment contract, they resolved to proceed with negotiations regarding the responsibilities of the position for the time being and revisit the issue of compensation at a later date.

→ to restructure/refinance a business or company

to recognize debt obligations by replacing or significantly modifying existing company debts, operations, or structure to eliminate financial harm and improve the business	The CEO of Hodak decided it was best to restructure the company after its bankruptcy.

→ to wind up a company

to formally bring a corporate entity to an end by selling all of its assets to pay off creditors	Winding up ABC Ltd may take up to three years.

→ to write off a company debt

to remove an asset or liability from accounting records and financial statements of a company because the assets are no longer available or valid	Unfortunately, they had to write off $3,000,000 of company debt.

4   Employment Law

A.   Key Legal Terms

a.   *Employment contract formation*

• *employment agreement* • *collective bargaining agreement* • *employee*	In addition to any contractual rights set forth in an *employment agreement* or *collective bargaining agreement,* many jurisdictions provide *employees* with certain statutory legal protections with respect to some aspects of the employment relationship.
• *compensation package* • *salary* • *bonus* • *pension-fund* • *employer* • *vacation time* • *at will* • *employment at will*	Employers may set out the terms and conditions of employment, including all aspects of the *compensation package,* in a written contract. A compensation package usually specifies the employee's *salary* or pay per month (or week), any *bonuses* the employee may be eligible to earn, any *pension-fund* or other matching contributions the *employer* may provide, and any *vacation* (**UK**: *holiday*) *time* to which the employee may be entitled. Note that employment contracts are much less common in the US than in many other countries. Absent an employment contract, employment relationships are generally *at will* in all US states except for Montana. *Employment at will* means that an employer can terminate an employee without notice for a good reason, a bad reason, or no reason at all, as long as the grounds for termination do not violate existing law or public policy (e.g. termination on discriminatory grounds).

| • *notice period* | In many civil law jurisdictions, an employment agreement may address the *notice period,* which states how far in advance the employee and the employer must give notice of his or its intent to terminate the employment relationship. Some jurisdictions also impose statutory requirements regarding minimum notice periods. |

When the employer discovered that John had embezzled corporate funds, it terminated his employment without notice and with immediate effect.

b.   *Employment contract termination*

• *termination* • *wrongful dismissal*	Either party may terminate an employment agreement at any time in accordance with a statutory or contractual notice period. A *termination* on grounds that are illegal or that violate public policy may constitute actionable *wrongful dismissal.*
• *constructive dismissal*	For *constructive dismissal* to exist, the employer must, without in fact terminating the employee, act in such a way that the employee reasonable considers himself or herself to have been dismissed and relieved of his or her employment duties.
• *serious misconduct* • *termination with immediate effect*	*Serious misconduct* by the employee (such as theft or operating machinery under the influence of alcohol) can lead to *termination with immediate effect.*

4

• *discrimination*	Actionable *discrimination* involves treating an employee less favorably than other, similarly situated, employees with regard to one or more aspects of his or her employment, on the basis of the employee's membership in a protected class (e.g. sex, gender, race, age, disability, national origin, certain genetic information).
• *protected periods*	The employer may not give notice of termination during certain *protected periods*. In some jurisdictions, such protections exist, for example, when an employee is on family, medical, or maternity leave.
• *bona fide occupational qualification*	A *bona fide occupational qualification* (**BFOQ**) may be a legitimate defense to a discrimination claim. A defendant might assert a **BFOQ** when, for example, it has chosen to consider only female candidates for a movie or theater role portraying a female character. Mere preferences, such as, for example, a condition that flight attendants be female to work for a particular airline because that airline caters primarily to male passengers who expect female flight attendants, would not qualify as a successful **BFOQ** defense.
• *layoff* • *mass layoff*	A *layoff* may involve a situation in which an employer shuts down or consolidates a particular segment of its operations, such that the employee's position or the need for an employee to work in a particular role no longer exists. A business that is in decline and sees itself forced to lay off a number of employees may conduct a *mass layoff*. Certain mass layoffs in the US require advance notice to employees pursuant to the **WARN** Act.

He is claiming *age discrimination*, as he learned that the company refused to hire him because it considered him, at age 47, too old to take on a customer-facing role.

c.   Employee rights

• *maternity leave*	In some jurisdictions, women may take *maternity leave* for a certain period of time following the birth (or in some cases, the adoption) of a child.
• *paternity leave*	*Paternity leave* for fathers following the birth (or in some cases, the adoption) of a child is less common than maternity leave.
• *non-compete clause*	To be enforceable, *non-compete clauses* must generally be reasonably limited with regard to duration, geographic scope, and the range and type of activity covered. Depending on the jurisdiction, financial compensation to the employee as consideration for the non-compete agreement may not always be necessary, but it may increase the likelihood that a court will consider a non-compete clause to be enforceable.

She did not disclose the fact that she was pregnant at the time of hiring, but will nevertheless be permitted to take *maternity leave*.

d.   Employment disputes

• *right to sue letter*	Before filing a lawsuit alleging employment discrimination, a plaintiff must usually first obtain a *right to sue letter* from the Equal Employment Opportunity Commission (EEOC).

• *strikes* • *picket* • *lock out*	As an action of last resort, and if other conditions apply (e.g. with support from a trade union), unionized employees can go on *strike* by refusing to work until the employer meets their demands. In the UK and the US, ununionized employees may also *picket* the premises of the employer to persuade others not to work or to attend the place of work. Employers in turn can *lock out* the employees by preventing access to the premises.
• *harassment*	*Harassment* is a form of employment discrimination characterized by unwelcome conduct on the basis of race, color, religion, national origin, sex, gender, age, disability, or certain genetic information. Harassment is unlawful when enduring the harassment becomes a condition of continued employment or where the harassing conduct creates a work environment that a reasonable person would find intimidating, hostile, or abusive.

e.   *Employee remedies*

• *reinstatement* • *compensation* • *exemplary/punitive damages*	Some jurisdictions may provide a remedy of *reinstatement* for an employee whom an employer has dismissed in an illegal manner. In such cases, the court may require the employer to reinstate the employee on the same terms governing the employee's prior employment. Many jurisdictions, however, do not offer reinstatement as a remedy, and courts cannot mandate that an employer reinstate a terminated employee. In such circumstances the employee's only remedy may be monetary – in other words financial *compensation* for certain losses resulting from the dismissal.

In especially aggravated cases of intentional discrimination, the plaintiff may seek *exemplary* or *punitive damages.*

B.   Sample Definitions

termination with immediate effect	Immediate end to an existing employment relationship.
non-compete clause	Provision of an employment contract that seeks to prohibit an employee, after termination of the contract, from carrying on an activity in competition with the former employer's business.

C.   Collocations Corner

→ to accuse of gross/serious misconduct

to allege that an employee has engaged in behavior that is wilfully or deliberately inconsistent with the law or with the terms and conditions of the employee's position	The bank accused John of gross misconduct after he stole money from his colleagues.

→ to apply for a position at/with

to make a formal application as a candidate for a position	He applied for a full-time position at one of the largest law firms in Zurich.

→ to be eligible for

| to qualify for something as a result of satisfying the appropriate conditions | Mark was eligible for a company car because he fulfilled the conditions of full-time employment and substantial work-related travel. |

→ to be under the influence of alcohol

| to have impaired judgment or functioning as a result of drinking alcohol | Please be aware that being under the influence of alcohol at work will lead to the termination of your contract, effective immediately. |

→ to claim constructive dismissal

| to assert that the employer, without in fact terminating the employee, has acted in such a way that the employee may consider himself or herself as having been dismissed | Terry claimed constructive dismissal after her boss severely restricted her areas of responsibility and her access to corporate files, forbade her from contacting clients, and left her without any real means of earning her commission. |

→ to comply with a notice period

| to adhere to the time period stipulated in the employment contract or in employment legislation stating how many weeks in advance an employee/ employer must inform the other about terminating employment | John complied with the notice period in his employment contract by formally giving notice to his employer four weeks before his last day of work. |

→ to comply with health and safety regulations

| to observe and adhere to sets of rules that ensure the health and safety of all employees at work | The CEO was responsible for complying with health and safety regulations. |

→ to discriminate against a person

to treat individuals differently with regard to the terms of their employment on the basis of their membership in a protected class, e.g. race, gender, age, religion	Tiffany argued that the partner of Maker AG discriminated against her on racial grounds, as he was only willing to hire Caucasians.

→ to draft company policies

to create an accessible set of principles and guidelines to regulate conduct within an organization	The company drafted an extensive list of policies, including policies on the use of social media at work.

→ to enter into an employment relationship with

to agree to take on an employment position with a particular employer	Norris Ltd. entered into an employment relationship with Mr. Marks for consulting services.

→ to extend an offer of employment

to offer someone employment at your organization	After the second round of interviews, the company extended an offer of employment to Bianca.

→ to fill a vacancy (UK)/an open position (US)

to appoint a person to hold an employment position that is currently available	The accounting firm hired Michelle to fill the open position it had advertised for weeks.

→ to give an employee notice of termination

to inform an employee that the employer is terminating the employee's employment (syn.: to dismiss, to discharge)	Pursuant to the employment agreement, the company gave notice of termination to all employees who had failed to meet their sales targets.

→ to give notice to the employer

| to inform your employer that you are resigning from your position | John decided to change industries and gave his employer three weeks' notice. |

→ to go on maternity/paternity leave

| to commence the period of absence from work that a mother/father may receive after the birth of a child | Tina went on maternity leave two months ago. |

→ to go on strike

| to refuse to attend or perform work in an attempt to force an employer to meet demands related to working conditions (often coordinated by a labor union) | Thirty employees of Gat Airways have gone on strike today, causing major flight delays. |

→ to hire an employee

| to employ someone for a paid position | After experiencing substantial growth, the company hired five more employees. |

→ to hold a position with

| to be employed in a particular field by a company or an individual | Brandon currently holds a position as a consultant with Haine Ltd. |

→ to negotiate a compensation package

| to discuss and reach an agreement with regard to employment benefits (e.g. salary, bonus, commission, insurance, stock ownership, relocation, or housing allowances) | Before drawing up the terms of the employment contract, the employer and employee had to negotiate a compensation package. |

→ to negotiate severance(US)/redundancy (UK) pay

| to discuss and reach an agreement on the amount an employer will pay to an employee upon the employee's dismissal or discharge from employment | Following the restructuring of the company, Dale negotiated the amount of severance pay he would receive. |

→ to recruit employees

| to search actively for the most suitable candidates for a position | The company is recruiting two employees for its new legal department. |

→ to work overtime

| to work in addition to one's regular working hours | Fred will not be working today, as he worked significant overtime this week. |

→ to resign from a position

| to voluntarily leave one's employment | Given his declining health, Mr. Hayes resigned from his position as Director of the NBS Bank. |

→ to sign a non-compete agreement

| to enter into a contractual agreement limiting an employee from working in a similar role for a competitor for a particular period of time (syn.: covenant not to complete, non-competition agreement) | William had to sign a non-compete clause before joining the company. |

→ to take/go on vacation

| to take advantage of a certain amount of paid time off work per year, to be used in any way the employee wishes | Bianca took a two-week vacation for her honeymoon in Brazil. |

I

4

→ to take disciplinary action

to change an employee's terms of employment or warn an employee of an impending change following the employee's unacceptable behavior or inadequate performance	The company took disciplinary action against William, putting him on notice that his employment was in jeopardy after he continued to act unprofessionally despite prior warnings.

→ to terminate a person's employment

to dismiss an employee from his or her position	After George received three warning notices about missing work without valid grounds, the Human Resources Manager terminated George's employment.

→ to work full-time/part time

to work a minimum number of hours as defined by one's employer or by employment legislation	Melissa used to work full-time but since having children she works on a part-time basis.

Personal Notes _____

_____

_____

_____

_____

_____

_____

5 Family Law

5

A. Key Legal Terms

• *marriage* • *spouse* • *husband/wife* • *annulment* • *divorce*	*Marriage* creates a certain legally recognized marital status between *spouses (husband or wife)*, and can be terminated by *annulment*, death, or *divorce*. Some countries recognize same-sex marriage.
• *irretrievable breakdown* • *irreconcilable differences* • *adultery* • *desertion*	Grounds for divorce vary by jurisdiction but can include *irretrievable (i.e. permanent) breakdown* or *irreconcilable differences* of marriage. Evidence of irretrievable breakdown may include *adultery, desertion*, or unreasonable behavior.
• *separation agreement*	If spouses no longer cohabit but do not want to petition for a divorce, they may enter into a *separation agreement*.
• *domestic partnership* • *dissolution order*	Domestic partners are same-sex couples who register their relationship and thereby obtain rights and obligations similar or analogous to those of married couples. To terminate the *domestic partnership*, one or both of the applicants can petition the court for a *dissolution order*.
• *prenuptial agreement*	Parties can enter into a *pre-nuptial agreement* to pre-determine the amounts that will be payable in the event of a later breakdown of marriage.
• *settlement agreement*	*A settlement agreement* sets out the rights and obligations of both parties to bring an end to a matrimonial dispute or litigation.

• *custody* • *parental responsibility*	*Custody* is the bundle of rights and responsibilities that parents have in relation to a child. This word has now been replaced in UK law by the term *parental responsibility*, which is self-explanatory.
• *minor children* • *rights of access/ visitation*	Where one parent has the day-to-day care and control of *minor children*, i.e. primary responsibility for them, *rights of access or visitation* for the other parent will need to be agreed upon between the parents or set out by court order. *Minor children* are often those under eighteen, depending on the jurisdiction.
• *maintain* • *maintenance* • *alimony*	A husband or wife is bound to *maintain* his or her spouse's standard of living (this is sometimes known as *alimony)*. Parents are obliged by law to *maintain* their minor children's standard of living. *Maintenance* is the provision of money, food, clothing, and other basic necessities of life.
• *abduction*	*Abduction* – taking or keeping a child under 16 from any person having lawful control of the child – is a criminal offense in many jurisdictions.
• *guardian*	A *guardian* is a person formally appointed by the court to look after a child's interests after the death of the child's parents, or if the parents are deemed unfit as guardians.
• *ward of the court*	A child can be made a *ward of the court*, whereupon the court will assume responsibility for that child's welfare. Courts have power to make certain orders to protect a child's interests.

She has filed for divorce (noun).

She intends to divorce him (verb).

She will be filing for a dissolution order (noun).

The civil partnership will be dissolved (verb).

The husband was ordered to pay child support to the mother to cover the costs of looking after both children, and in turn, the husband was given the right to regular access.

Mr. X was appointed as guardian to Y after the death of both Y's parents.

Child Z was removed from her single mother's control and, for Z's safety, was made a ward of the court.

B.   Sample Definitions

separation agreement	Contract between spouses that regulates the consequences of deciding to live separate lives.
alimony (US); maintenance	Regular financial support contributions that the payer is legally bound to make to the recipient.
parental responsibility	Rights and obligations of parents toward their children: parents are responsible for their children's upbringing, education, legal representation, and the administration of their children's assets for the children's benefit.

C.   Collocations Corner

→ to appoint a guardian

to choose a guardian, i.e. a person who assumes a legal obligation to look after the well-being of a ward, for a person who cannot look after himself because of his age, mental or physical status, or other limiting condition	The judge appointed Mary to act as the child's guardian because both of the child's parents were in prison.

→ to assume responsibility for

to take on a role that imposes accountability for something or someone	As her mother was a drug addict, Stella became legally emancipated and also assumed responsibility for her younger siblings.

→ to award alimony to

to grant the right to receive financial support from a spouse for a certain period of time after separation or divorce (Syn.: maintenance)	The court awarded alimony to Mark's ex-wife in the amount of $2,000.00 per month.

→ to divorce one's spouse

to dissolve one's marriage legally	She divorced her husband after five years of marriage.

→ to enter into a civil partnership

to register, under the law, a relationship between partners of the same sex, which gives each party certain rights and obligations	He entered into a civil partnership with his boyfriend of ten years.

→ to enter into a marriage/marital relationship

to promise legally, by way of contract, to live together in a lawful relationship for life or until the legal termination of the relationship Entering into a marital relationship changes both parties' marital status, giving each party new rights and obligations.	After a long engagement period, they entered into a marriage.

→ to file for a dissolution order

to submit a petition to the court requesting the end to a marriage or to any legally formalized agreement	Everyone could see that she was unhappy in her marriage, so no one was surprised when she filed for a dissolution order.

→ to have a right of access

to have the right to see one's children, usually following a divorce or separation, to have permission or authorization to enter a place or to retrieve files or data from a computer	Following the divorce, the non-custodial parent often retains rights of access to the children, meaning that parent can visit the children or take them on excursions.

→ to have care and control of

to have the authority to make important decisions for someone, usually because of that person's age, mental or physical status, or other limiting condition	As the children's legal guardian, I have care and control over Mark, whom I now consider to be my own child.

→ to have custody of

| to receive the right of care, control, and maintenance of a child following a divorce or separation proceeding | Following her divorce from John, Jessica had custody of their child. |

→ to have joint custody of

| to share legal and physical rights of the child as a result of a court order and a physical custody schedule distributing parenting tasks and duties | Although Nicky and Tim had joint custody of their child, they could not agree on a physical custody schedule. |

→ to make a child a ward of the court

| to assign, by law, a legal guardian for a child exposed to danger at home, or to assign the child to a foster home to keep him or her safe | As the child was at risk of experiencing domestic violence, the guardian ad litem submitted a request to the court to make the child a ward of the court. |

→ to pay maintenance

| to provide alimony or other financial support for living expenses to a former spouse for a certain period of time after a divorce | As he had just lost his job, he was no longer able to pay maintenance to his former wife. |

→ to petition for a divorce

| to submit a formal application to an authority or a court for the dissolution of a marriage | His wife has no idea that he petitioned for a divorce. |

→ to pre-determine an amount

to determine an amount beforehand, usually in the context of a divorce, separation, or other legal dispute	It was important to the young woman that her lawyer pre-determine the amount of alimony her former husband would pay before she agreed to move out of the family home.

→ to share custody of

to have legal and physical custody of the child as a single unit, cooperating together instead of having responsibilities divided by the court	Jessica and John shared custody of Mark and cooperated in handling their responsibilities as parents.
to equally divide the time spent with the child between each parent in the case of a separation or divorce	

Personal Notes _____

_____

_____

_____

_____

_____

_____

6 Trusts and Estates/ Inheritance Law

A. Key Legal Terms

a. Inheritance

• *inheritance* • *succession* • *estate* • *probate* • *will* • *a grant of probate*	*Inheritance* law (referred to in some jurisdictions as the law of *succession*) governs the distribution of an individual's estate, i.e. the assets subject to *probate* (the legal process for validating a person's *will*) upon his or her death. Under common law, property held in joint accounts is not included in the deceased's estate. Only once *a grant of probate* has been received from the probate authorities may the estate be administered. Some jurisdictions, however, do not require a grant of probate because following the decedent's death, his or her legal heirs immediately receive control of the decedent's assets and liabilities.
• *legacy* • *devise* • *moveable assets* • *immoveable assets*	Technically, a *legacy* is a gift of personal property or money, and a devise a gift of real property from the decedent's estate. Jurisdictions differ on whether inheritance law distinguishes between transferring *moveable assets* (personal property) and transferring *immoveable assets* (real property).
• *codicil*	A will may be amended in writing by a *codicil*.

• *intestate* • *kinship* • *domicile*	A person who dies without leaving a valid will is said to have died *intestate*. The decedent's assets are disposed of according to each jurisdiction's conventions and statutory provisions governing succession (e.g. spouse, children, and other relatives according to the degree of *kinship*) and *domicile*.
• *statutory entitlements* • *forced heirship rights/compulsory shares* • *disposable assets* • *testation*	In some civil law jurisdictions, mandatory *statutory entitlements* known as *forced heirship rights* (or *compulsory shares*) arise regardless of whether or not a person died intestate. Only once these compulsory shares have been satisfied may any remaining *assets* be *disposed of* according to a person's wishes. In other words, forced heirship rights limit the freedom to transfer property by will *(testation)*.
• *contract of succession* • *inheritance agreement* • *family contract* • *trust*	In these civil law jurisdictions, forced heirship rights may be modified or overridden by a *contract of succession* or *inheritance agreement*. Under US law, a person may also dispose of assets by means of a *trust*. While trusts do not exist in many civil law jurisdictions, these jurisdictions may recognize and acknowledge the existence of valid trusts under foreign law.

A foreign national *domiciled* in a particular country may in his will elect to have the law of his own country of citizenship govern *succession* to his estate.

b.   *Legal personnel*

• *deceased* • *decedent* • *issue* • *descendants* • *testator* • *testatrix* • *executor* • *personal representative*	A person who has died is known as the *deceased* or the *decedent*. The *issue* of the deceased (i.e. his or her children and children's children etc.) are the *descendants*. If the deceased left a will, he or she is referred to as the *testator* or *testatrix* respectively (although the latter term is now largely obsolete). In many cases a testator appoints an *executor* (or *personal representative*) to execute the testator's will.
• *beneficiary* • *devisee* • *legatee* • *heir* • *ancestor* • *appointed heirs* • *statutory heirs*	The term *beneficiary* covers both *devisees* (US/UK: beneficiaries who receive real property according to the terms of the will), and *legatees* (US/UK: beneficiaries who receive money or other personal property). Originally, the term *heir* was confined to the deceased's descendants and closest relatives who acquired real property from an *ancestor* who died intestate. Today however, the term commonly refers to any individual who succeeds to property, either by will or law. The law may distinguish between *appointed heirs* (who receive an inheritance under a will) and *statutory heirs* (who receive an inheritance under the rules of forced heirship or intestacy).
• *surviving spouse* • *predeceased*	The *surviving spouse* is the husband or wife who survives or outlives the other; the *predeceased* is a person (typically related by blood or marriage) who dies before the testator.

• *witness*	In some jurisdictions, wills and inheritance agreements are only valid if they have been signed in the presence of *witnesses* who must attest (confirm in writing or in a public deed) that the testator signed the will in their presence.
• *trustee* • *beneficiary*	If the testator sets up a trust (US/UK), the appointed *trustee(s)* will manage the trust and its assets for the benefit of the *beneficiaries*.
• *administrator* • *letters of administration*	In the US and many common law jurisdictions, the representative of an intestate estate is called an *administrator*. While a grant of probate is obtained by executors of a will, the administrator is granted *letters of administration* authorizing disposal of the deceased's assets. The executor's or administrator's duties include discharging the funeral expenses, the costs of obtaining probate or letters of administration distributing assets to the heirs, and settling any outstanding debts of the deceased.
• *Letter Testamentary* • *inheritance certificate*	The court or other probate authority may issue a document known as a *Letter Testamentary* or *inheritance certificate* entitling the heir(s) or beneficiaries to manage the deceased's assets jointly for a temporary period of time.

The *decedent's* business assets have been valued for *probate*.

c.   *Terms of the will*

6

• *bequest* • *bequeath* • *devise*	In the US/UK, personal property given under the provisions of a will is known as a *bequest*; "*bequeath*" is the verb form meaning "to make a bequest." To give real estate is to *devise*.
• *inter vivos*	A gift made during the giver's lifetime is referred to as an *inter vivos* gift.
• *disinherited*	A spouse or descendant who is expressly excluded from benefitting under a will is said to have been disinherited. Many civil law jurisdictions, which impose a statutory minimum share of the testator's estate to the surviving spouse and children, do not permit a testator to disinherit these heirs. Nevertheless, in some cases, an heir may be *disinherited* for committing a serious offense against the testator or a person closely connected to the testator, or for a serious violation of family law.
• *action in abatement/action for reduction* • *claw back*	In some civil law jurisdictions, heirs who do not receive the full value of their statutory entitlement may bring an *action in abatement/action for reduction* to *claw back* their statutory share.

He left generous *bequests* to his scientific colleagues. She *bequeathed* her entire collection of engravings to the national art gallery.

d. Interests in real property

• *joint tenancy* • *tenants in common*	In many common law jurisdictions including the UK and parts of the US, jointly owned property *(joint tenancy)* passes automatically to the surviving joint owner separately from any will (hence avoiding probate); consequently, the deceased joint owner's interest cannot be inherited by his or her heirs. *Tenants in common*, on the other hand, hold an individual, undivided ownership interest in the property where each party has the right to dispose of his or her ownership interest by will.
• *life estate* • *life interest* • *usufruct* • *life tenant*	A *life estate* (also known as a *life interest* or *usufruct rights*) involves the right to use or occupy real property for the lifetime of the *life tenant*.

His mother was *granted* a *life estate* in the family home.

e. Taxes

• *inheritance tax/ estate tax*	In the US/UK, once the competent authorities are satisfied that duties (in the form of *inheritance taxes*, or *estate taxes*) have been paid on those parts of the estate (if any) subject to such duties, the heirs may dispose of the estate. In civil law jurisdictions, liability for inheritance taxes may rest with the heirs or with the estate.

The transfer had been executed in an attempt to avoid *estate taxes*.

B.   Sample Definitions

trust	Special legal arrangement in which a settlor transfers ownership of certain assets to one or more trustees who are required to administer and make use of the assets for the benefit of one or more beneficiaries.
inheritance certificate	Official document listing all the persons entitled to inherit, confirming a person's status as an heir.

C.   Collocations Corner

→ to administer an estate

to manage assets of a deceased, e.g. paying the decedent's debts and distributing assets	Mr. Rose administered the estate of Dr. White.

→ to appoint an executor

to imbue a person with the authority to dispose of certain assets under the will	Dr. White appointed his son as executor of his will.

→ to attest to the authenticity of

to certify formally that something, e.g. a will, is original and genuine	The lawyer attested to the authenticity of Dr. White's will.

→ to be of sound mind

to be legally deemed to have the capacity to reason and think independently	Dr. White was not of sound mind in the weeks leading up to his death.

→ to challenge a will

to make a legal claim as a beneficiary, e.g. for improper execution of the will, lack of sound mind, or fraud	Two of the beneficiaries challenged the will on the grounds that their father was not of sound mind at the time of writing the will.

→ to contest a will

to make a legal claim as a beneficiary, e.g. for improper execution of the will, lack of sound mind, or fraud	The deceased's daughter contested the will on the grounds of fraud.

→ to deprive someone of something

to take something away or withhold something	Dr. White deprived his children of receiving shares in his business.

→ to discharge a debt

to be released from liability to creditors	The bank discharged Dr. White's debts upon his death.

→ to dispose of assets

to sell or distribute assets	The executor disposed of Dr. White's assets.

→ to draw up a will

to draft a will	His lawyer drew up a will for him.

→ to endow a foundation

to establish an institution by way of donation, e.g. a charitable organization	In his will, Dr. White endowed an educational foundation.

→ to execute a will

to perform legal requirements which make a will binding, e.g. signing in the presence of witnesses	The lawyer executed Dr. White's will in the witnesses' presence.

→ to grant probate

to be given official authority to administer an estate, resolve debts, and dispose of assets	The Probate Officer granted probate to the executor of Dr. White's will.

→ to impose taxes

| to require individuals or companies to pay tax | The government plans to impose higher inheritance taxes. |

→ to issue a certificate

| to provide an official document attesting a fact, e.g. a death certificate | The coroner issued a death certificate upon Dr. White's death. |

→ to lack testamentary capacity

| to have insufficient legal and mental ability to make or alter a will | Dr. White lacked testamentary capacity at the time of altering his will. |

→ to make a claim

| to assert a right to a sum of the estate in a will | He made a claim for 10% more of Dr. White's estate. |

→ to perform duties

| to carry out one's legal obligations | The Executor performed his duties by disposing of the relevant assets. |

→ to read out the will

| to officially disclose the terms of the will to the heirs | The Executor read out Dr. White's will to his heirs. |

→ to revoke a will

| to rescind one's will at any time before death | Dr. White revoked his will two months before his death. |

→ to vest power in

| to give someone authority or rights to perform certain acts | The will vested power in the Executor to dispose of Dr. White's estate. |

→ to witness a will

| to observe and verify the signing of a will so as to ensure its validity | The lawyer, along with Mr. Jinn's accountant, witnessed Mr. Jinn's will. |

I

6

7   Insurance Law

A.   Key Legal Terms

a.   *The insurance relationship*

• *insurer* • *insurance carrier* • *insurance company* • *insurance policy* • *policyholder* • *insured party* • *insured* • *coverage* • *covered events* • *claimant* • *insurance proceeds* • *beneficiary* • *third-party* *beneficiary*	The *insurer,* also known as the *insurance carrier* or the *insurance company*, issues an *insurance policy* to the *policyholder*, also known as the *insured party* or *insured*. The insured and the policyholder can, but need not be, identical. The insurer provides *coverage* for certain acts, omissions, or similar *covered events* specified in the policy. When the policyholder or insured brings a claim under the policy, he or she is referred to as the *claimant*. For covered claims, the insurer pays the *insurance proceeds* to the claimant, who may be the policyholder or insured himself or a designated *third-party beneficiary*.
• *underwriters* • *underwriting* *guidelines* • *insurance premium* • *insurance adjuster* • *loss adjuster* • *claims adjuster*	Insurers rely on *underwriters*, who apply certain *underwriting guidelines* to evaluate the possible exposure under a new policy, to determine how much coverage to offer, and to set the *insurance premium*. *Insurance adjusters*, also known as *loss adjusters* in the UK, or as *claims adjusters*, investigate claims under an insurance policy by speaking with the claimant and any witnesses, as well as reviewing relevant records and any tangible objects at issue.

The company took out an insurance policy for its subsidiary, and named itself as the beneficiary of any insurance proceeds which the insurer would pay if a covered event occurred.

b.   Common types of insurance

- *general liability insurance*
- *commercial general liability (CGL) policy*
- *directors' and officers' liability insurance (D&O)*

A *general liability* policy covers different insurable risks, including financial losses resulting from claims against the insured (based on injury or property damage resulting from the insured's direct or indirect actions). Businesses operating in the litigious US environment often obtain a *commercial general liability (CGL) policy* covering many insurable risks, as well as *directors' and officers' (D&O) liability insurance*. D&O insurance indemnifies a company's directors and officers for losses or defense costs in lawsuits alleging that they committed wrongful acts in their corporate roles.

- *life insurance policy*
- *disability insurance*
- *workers' compensation insurance*

Under a *life insurance policy*, known as life assurance in the UK, the insurer pays a designated beneficiary (usually a family member of the policyholder) a sum of money upon the death of the policyholder. *Disability insurance* also provides for certain short-term or long-term payments, usually in installments, if a policyholder is unable to work and earn an income as a result of an accident, illness, or other disabling event. In states which do not require employers to provide paid sick days, employees may use their disability insurance benefits to cover time missed from work for health reasons. Finally, *workers' compensation insurance* provides medical benefits or wage replacement payments to US employees injured or killed in the course of their employment, in return for an agreement not to sue.

• *homeowners' insurance (HOI)* • *home insurance* • *renters' insurance* • *title insurance*	In the US, *homeowners' insurance (HOI)* or *home insurance* applies to residential homes, and usually covers losses from damage to the home or possessions inside the home, damages from loss of the home, and often also liability for accidents inside the home. *Renters' insurance* provides similar coverage, but does not cover losses relating to the residence itself. *Title insurance* covers financial losses resulting from defects in title to real property.
• *vehicle insurance* • *car insurance* • *third-party liability* • *fully comprehensive insurance* • *partially comprehensive insurance*	*Vehicle* or *car insurance* covers the owner, primary driver(s), and occasionally other drivers of a road vehicle for *third-party liability* from accidents. It can take the form of *fully comprehensive insurance*, which covers all damage and liability incurred in connection with the insured vehicle, or *partially comprehensive insurance*, which covers only portions of damage and liability so incurred.
• *professional liability insurance* • *malpractice insurance* • *errors and omissions (E&O) insurance*	Physicians, lawyers, accountants, brokers, and other professional service providers may carry *professional liability insurance* policies, also known as *malpractice insurance* or *errors and omissions (E&O) insurance* policies. Coverage takes effect only when the policyholder/insured is sued by a client alleging negligence in the performance of professional services, and generally does not extend to criminal prosecution. In the US, malpractice insurance is mandatory for physicians and lawyers.

The lawsuit alleging that the corporation's CEO committed fraud while acting in his corporate role triggered coverage under the directors' and officers' liability policy.

c.   *Concepts under the policy*

• *occurrence-based policy* • *claims-made policy*	An *occurrence-based policy* covers losses from covered events occurring during the policy period, even if the full extent of the loss does not become apparent until after the policy period has expired. By contrast, a *claims-made policy* covers claims made during the policy period. To trigger coverage, the policyholder must report to the insurer any claims arising during the policy period, even those not yet ripened into a lawsuit. Claims-made policies allow insurers to limit their long-term liability, as they generally do not provide coverage if the policyholder fails to report a claim during the policy period.
• *deductible* • *policy limits* • *aggregate limit* • *retained limit* • *self-insured retention (SIR)* • *exclusions* • *exhaustion* • *excess insurance policy* • *umbrella policy* • *drop-down coverage*	Most insurance policies specify a *deductible*, which the policyholder pays out of pocket, and which applies either to each covered incident or on an annual basis. Policies also specify the *policy limits* or the *aggregate limit*, which is the maximum benefit an insurer will pay during the policy period. To reduce their premiums, policyholders may choose a policy with a *retained limit*, also known as a *self-insured retention (SIR)*, which operates like a deductible. Insurance policies also contain specific *exclusions* for events for which the insurer will not provide coverage. After an insurer pays out all possible amounts under a policy, coverage is *exhausted*. Exhausting coverage under a policy may trigger coverage under an *excess insurance policy*. An *umbrella policy* also provides additional protection, as it covers some of the same risks as the underlying policy, and can *"drop down"* to fill gaps in coverage.

- *right of subrogation*
- *reinsurance*
- *reinsurer*
- *reinsurance premium*
- *reinsurance agreement*
- *reinsurance company*

When an insurance company acquires a *right of subrogation* for a policyholder's claim, the insurance company acquires the legal right to pursue recovery on behalf of the policyholder. An insurer can also purchase *reinsurance* from a *reinsurer* by paying a *reinsurance premium* and entering into a *reinsurance agreement* specifying the conditions upon which the reinsurer will pay a share of the claims for which the insurance company is liable to its policyholders. The reinsurer can be a specialist *reinsurance company* or another primary insurance company.

After coverage under the primary policy was exhausted, the insured made a claim for coverage under its *excess insurance policy*.

Personal Notes _____

_____

_____

_____

_____

_____

_____

_____

d.   Concepts under the law

- *duty to indemnify*
- *duty to defend*
- *duty to pay*

Depending on the type of insurance coverage, an insurer may have a *duty to indemnify* its policyholders, which means that the insurer must pay a judgment against the policyholder up to policy limits if the judgment results from a covered event. The *duty to defend* describes an insurer's obligation to provide its policyholders with a legal defense to covered claims, which includes selecting defense counsel and paying all legal bills. To trigger this duty, the policyholder must generally only establish that there is a potential for coverage under the policy. As a result, the duty to defend applies even where coverage is initially unclear and ultimately may not exist. *Duty to pay* policies do not include language specifying that the insurer has a duty to defend. Such policies only require the insurer to reimburse the policyholder for amounts spent in defending a claim.

- *duty of good faith and fair dealing*
- *good faith*
- *insurance bad faith*

Under the law of most US jurisdictions, but not under UK law, insurance companies owe *a duty of good faith and fair dealing*. The duty is imputed to every insurance contract. If the insurer fails to act in *good faith*, the policyholder may bring a tort claim for breach or for *insurance bad faith*, for which punitive damages may be available. Insurance bad faith includes undue delay in handling claims, improper or inadequate investigation, refusal to acknowledge a claim, refusal to defend a lawsuit, refusal to make a reasonable settlement offer, threats against a policyholder, or unreasonable interpretations of a policy.

As the insurer refused to defend the lawsuit on behalf of its insured, the insured brought a claim against the insurer for *bad faith* and breach of the *duty of good faith and fair dealing.*

B.   Sample Definitions

coverage	Amount/scope of risk covered by way of insurance.
exclusions	Terms in an insurance policy that seek to restrict the rights of the policyholder/insured by defining events for which the insurer will not provide coverage.
insurance bad faith	In the US, a claim in tort that a policyholder may bring against an insurance company for a violation of good faith in order to obtain punitive damages if the insurance company's conduct was particularly reprehensible.

Personal Notes _____

_____

_____

_____

_____

_____

C. Collocations Corner

→ to act in bad/good faith

to have good and honest intentions or malicious and dishonest intentions, regardless of the actions taken	The judges assessed whether the insurer acted in good faith in denying coverage for the claim.

→ to admit coverage

to acknowledge that the event or loss which occurred is within the scope of the insured's policy	The insurance company admitted coverage after the insured submitted his claim.

→ to ascertain coverage

to establish and clarify the scope of the insured's policy	The insurer had to ascertain coverage before paying out on the insured's claim.

→ to assess coverage

to evaluate and determine the scope of an insurance policy	The insurer denied insurance proceeds after assessing the insured party's coverage.

→ to assume the defense

to be required to provide policyholders with a legal defense for covered claims, including selecting defense counsel and covering legal fees	The insurer had to assume the defense of the insured by covering his legal bills.

→ to be covered against a loss

to be protected against certain acts, omissions, or similar events specified in an insurance policy, so that if these acts or events transpire, the insured party will suffer minimal or no losses	The couple was covered against theft.

→ to be liable under the policy for

| to be legally responsible or accountable for something based on the terms of the insurance policy | The insurer was liable under the policy for proceedings against the insured in relation to covered claims. |

→ to benefit under the policy

| to receive discounted and/ or free services under an insurance policy | Ms. Day will benefit under her insurance policy, as she will receive contributions towards vaccinations. |

→ to bring a claim for coverage under the policy

| to assert or argue formally that a certain claim falls within the scope of the insurance policy and is therefore covered | The insured brought a claim for coverage under the policy on the basis that the injury had occurred at his home. |

→ to carry insurance

| to have insurance | She could not afford the treatment because she did not carry health insurance. |

→ to choose counsel from a panel of preferred firms

| to be permitted to choose a firm for representation from a given list | The insured was allowed to choose counsel from a panel of preferred firms, rather than choosing her sister as her lawyer. |

→ to choose coverage counsel

| to have the express right to decide on an attorney of the insured's choice | The insured was permitted to choose coverage counsel for the proceedings against him. |

→ to deny coverage

| to reject an insurance claim on the basis that the event falls outside the scope of the policy | The insurance company denied coverage for damaged goods. |

→ **to determine coverage**

to establish the scope of events or losses covered by a certain policy	The insurance company had to determine coverage under her policy before issuing her proceeds.

→ **to draft a policy on a claims-made basis**

to draft a policy stating that the insurer will pay out a claim during the policy period irrespective of when the loss or event occurred	The insurance company drafted a professional indemnity policy for the solicitor on a claims-made basis.

→ **to draft a policy on an occurrence basis**

to draft a policy stating that the insurer will pay proceeds for events or losses that actually occur during the policy period, even if the full extent of the loss does not become apparent until after the policy period has expired	The insurance company drafted the employer's liability insurance on an occurrence basis.

→ **to exhaust coverage**

to receive all possible amounts under a policy	Ms. Rose exhausted coverage after receiving $2 million under her insurance policy.

→ **to fill gaps in coverage**

to cover for events and losses that fall outside the scope of one's insurance coverage, e.g. by taking out supplemental policies	The supplemental insurance package will fill gaps in her coverage related to dental care.

→ **to find coverage**

to find that a policy covers certain losses, occurrences, or claims	The insurer found coverage for accidental loss and damage.

→ to have coverage for

to be protected against certain events within a defined scope by way of insurance	She had coverage for accidental injury.

→ to investigate claims under the policy

to determine whether a claim to an insurer falls within the scope of the policy, and whether the facts underlying the claim are true	The insurance company investigated Mr. Green's claim under the policy and rejected it for lack of evidence.

→ to issue a coverage determination

to put forth, as the insurer, a written statement on whether a policy covers a loss, occurrence, or claim	The insurer issued a coverage determination regarding the elective surgical procedure.

→ to issue an insurance policy to

to supply an insured party with an insurance policy	The company issued Mr. Ford an insurance policy covering the risk of accidental injury.

→ to make a claim under the policy

to bring a claim in an attempt to receive compensation for loss resulting from an event covered under the policy	Ms. Hall made a claim under the policy after having to pay hospital fees.

→ to obtain insurance on/for

to purchase an insurance policy	The family obtained travel insurance for their upcoming summer trip.

→ to offer coverage for

to provide the possibility to protect against certain events specified in an insurance policy	The insurance company offered coverage for stolen goods.

→ to pay the insurance premium

to periodically pay an amount to the insurance company for covering their risk	Mr. Jones paid the insurance premium monthly.

→ to pay the insurance proceeds

to pay a sum of money to the insured party for a covered claim	The company paid the insurance proceeds to the claimant after he successfully claimed coverage for theft of his computer.

→ to pay policy limits

to pay the maximum amount of money to the insured following a claim	The insurer paid the maximum policy limits of $10,000 to the insured following the insured's accident.

→ to provide coverage

to provide insurance for a defined scope of risk	The company provided coverage for natural disasters.

→ to receive insurance proceeds

to receive a sum of money from an insurer for covered claims	The claimant received insurance proceeds for her loss of luggage claim.

→ to take out insurance on/for

to contract with an insurance company to cover against losses resulting from specified events	He took out life insurance for himself and his wife.

→ to take out a policy on/for

to contract with an insurance company to cover oneself against certain risks	My friend took out a policy for travel insurance.

→ to trigger coverage under the policy

to prompt a policy to cover loss and liability	Her injury triggered coverage under the insurance policy.

8   Intellectual Property Law

A.   Key Legal Terms

a.   *General*

• *intangible assets*	Intellectual Property (IP) refers to creations of the mind. IP results from the expression of an idea, and IP law then grants the owners exclusive rights to a number of *intangible assets*. The intangible assets include two broad categories – industrial property and artistic, literary, and musical works – so IP might be a brand, an invention, a design, a phrase, a symbol, a song, or another intellectual creation.
• *copyright* • *trademarks* • *patents* • *industrial designs* • *trade secrets*	IP rights can include *copyright, trademarks, patents, industrial designs*, and *trade secrets*, depending on the jurisdiction. IP law allows people to own the work that they create and to license and control the use or reproduction of such work. One stated objective of IP law is to promote progress in society by offering certain exclusive rights to artists and inventors and so encouraging them to create and disclose their works. IP law also offers a financial incentive for the cost of research and development to discover and develop new drugs for medical use.

8

• *abstract*	The *abstract* quality of the property rights involved in IP presents a contrast to the nature of rights attached to tangible property that cannot be as readily reproduced or shared.
• *infringement* • *injunctions* • *damages* • *account of profits*	Enforcement proceedings can be used to take action against *infringement* of IP rights. Such actions can lead to *injunctions, damages,* and an *account of profits* (which means disclosing any income made from the alleged infringement).

Intellectual Property law continues to expand. In some countries patents have been granted on human genes and biotechnology, raising the potential for infringement lawsuits.

Personal Notes _____

_____

_____

_____

_____

_____

_____

_____

b. *Copyright*

8

• *automatically*	Copyright is a legal right that comes into existence *automatically* (that is without registration) in original literary, musical, dramatic, or artistic works as expressed in sound recordings, films, broadcasts, and the typography of published works. Machine-readable computer software has been given the copyright status of literary works in most jurisdictions.
• *material form* • *original*	The work must exist in *material form* – in other words it is not just an idea – and it must be *original* in that it has individual character.
• *partial monopoly* • *right of fair use*	Copyright gives the authors the "right to copy" which means that they can control reproduction, as well as determining who can perform or adapt the work, and who in addition to the author can derive financial benefit from the work. The author can also require receiving credit for the work. Copyright can be said to bestow only a *partial monopoly* on the authors, as there are various exceptions when copying will be allowed without infringing the rights of the author. Such an exception is the *right of fair use* under US law.
• *duration*	The *duration* of copyright varies by jurisdiction, type of work, and nature of authorship. For some works, copyright protection may last for the life of the author plus 70 years, while other works may enjoy copyright protection for 95 years from first publication or 120 years from creation. Different rules for the duration of copyright protection may apply to works made for hire.

• *piracy*	*Piracy* is the illegal use of material that is protected by copyright and in certain jurisdictions gives rise to criminal liability as well as civil remedies.
• *public domain* • *royalties*	Where copyright protection has expired, the work is said to be in the *public domain,* which must be distinguished from being publicly available – on the internet for example – but still subject to copyright protection.

Royalties are payments by a party, e.g. a licensee, to the owner of an intellectual property asset, e.g. a song or a book, for the right to use that asset. |

To overcome the logistical difficulty of enforcing individual copyright licenses, collecting societies and performing rights organizations collect the *royalties* arising on thousands of works at once.

Personal Notes _____

_____

_____

_____

_____

_____

_____

c. *Patent law*

• *invent* • *useful* • *not obvious*	A patent is a right granted by registration of the patent to anyone who *invents* something that is *new*, *useful*, and *not obvious*.
• *exclusive right* • *patent license* • *patent pending*	Registration allows the inventor or owner of the patent to exploit the *exclusive right* to the patent for a limited time in exchange for the public disclosure of the information. This exclusive right allows the patent owner to prevent others from manufacturing, using, or selling the invention without permission (in the form of a *patent license*). When a patent is applied for but not yet granted, the words *"patent pending"* are used to place others on notice even though the patent is not enforceable prior to registration.
• *civil lawsuits* • *Patent Office*	Most patents have a maximum duration of 20 years from the filing date of the earliest US or international application to which priority is claimed. For US patent applications filed before or in force in June 1995, the patent term is either 17 years from the issue date or 20 years from the filing date of the earliest US or international application to which priority is claimed. After the patent's term, the patent expires automatically without the option of extension or renewal. Enforcement of patent rights is through *civil lawsuits* that seek damages for past infringement, and an injunction to prohibit future acts of infringement. Countries will normally establish their own *Patent Office* to grant patents and to operate the country's patent laws, but enforcement will be through the national courts.

8

- *patent prosecution*
- *prior art*

There are various types of patents, including biological, chemical, pharmaceutical, and business method patents. The cost of obtaining a patent, referred to as *patent prosecution,* and the maintenance of the same patent can be significant. The creators or originators of inventions can instead establish their identity by publishing a detailed description of the invention without patenting it and in so doing attempt to establish *prior art* in order to prevent others from later patenting the same invention.

An early grant of a patent-related license in the US involved a right granted in the mid-1600s to the exclusive use, for ten years, of a new process for making salt.

Personal Notes _____

d.   *Trademark law*

8

- *distinguishing mark*
- *symbol*
- *design*
- *image*
- *logo*
- *shape*

A trademark is a *distinguishing mark* or sign that establishes the identity of goods or services. A trademark can be a word, a phrase, a *symbol*, a sound, a *design*, an *image*, a *logo*, or any combination of these. Trademarks can include three-dimensional *shapes*.

- *unregistered mark*
- *distinctive*
- *descriptive*
- *deceptive*

In the US, even *unregistered marks* enjoy some federal statutory protection, in that the holder of an unregistered mark can avail himself of a statutory civil cause of action for claims of false designation of origin and false advertising. Registered trademarks benefit from advantages over unregistered marks. For a mark to be eligible for trademark protection, it must be used in commerce and it must be *distinctive*. The requirement of distinctiveness addresses a trademark's ability to identify and distinguish particular goods as those of one producer or source rather than another. An inherently distinctive mark is not a word found in a dictionary as it has no prior meaning. A *descriptive* mark that uses words is more difficult to register, and certain marks may not be registrable if they include flags or emblems or are *deceptive* as to the country of origin of the goods.

- *objections*
- *register*
- *renewed*

The registration process will take a number of months or longer if *objections* to the new mark are filed with the trademark office.

Once registered, a mark will be held on the *register* for an initial period (e.g. ten years in the US and the UK) and can then be *renewed* for a further period or periods.

The application filing and renewal process is usually undertaken by trademark agents who first carry out a search for prior rights, and who also consider the appropriate class of goods or services and any further filings to ensure international protection.

The shape of the Coca Cola bottle and the three-pronged Mercedes Benz star are examples of three-dimensional shapes that have been registered as trademarks in addition to the distinctive and descriptive marks of the corporate owners.

e.   *International IP*

• *innovation*	The World Intellectual Property Organization (WIPO) is a United Nations agency dedicated to the use of IP as a means to stimulate *innovation* and creativity.
• *resolution of IP disputes*	WIPO offers international protection of IP and specifically provides the framework and systems to make it easier to obtain registration internationally for patents, trademarks, and designs. Given that WIPO represents 185 member states, which is 90 percent of the countries worldwide, international IP issues are well coordinated. WIPO also provides mechanisms for the *resolution of IP disputes* and continues to develop the international legal IP framework.

I

8

- *domain names*
- *internet protocol*
- *registrars*

Domain names are another important area of **IP**. Each domain name represents an *internet protocol* or, in simple terms, is the internet address for websites and other internet participants. Domain names are regulated in accordance with the Domain Name System which is in turn controlled by the Internet Corporation for Assigned Names and Numbers (**ICANN**) which manages the top-level development and architecture of the internet domain name space. It authorizes domain name *registrars* who sell their services to the public and through whom domain names may be registered and reassigned.

One other mechanism to provide international coordination of IP law is the law of the European Union. Trademarks, for example, may be registered within individual countries, or across the whole of the EU (by means of a Community Trademark.)

- *harmonization*

Within EU member states, national law is required to implement the EU Directives so that the law in each jurisdiction is more or less equivalent, the eventual goal being *harmonization* of trademark law within the EU.

Domain names provide easily recognized and memorable letters for numerically addressed internet resources.

B. Sample Definitions

intangible assets	Asset that has no physical substance.
public domain	Legal sphere in which rights are freely available to the public as a whole and cannot be privately owned.
royalties	Payments made by a licensee in return for the right to use intellectual property.

C. Collocations Corner

→ to advise on the availability of trademarks/trade names

to provide information on whether trade names can be registered based on current trademarks/names listed in a database	The Trademark Office advised the company on the availability of the trade name "Testlé."

→ to apply for registration of a patent

to request the grant of a patent for the invention described and claimed by the applicant	Derrick applied for registration of a patent for his latest invention.

→ to control reproduction

to prevent others from copying protected work without authorization	The author of the book had the right to control reproduction of his work to prevent others from copying it.

→ to copyright work

to grant to the creator of a piece of original, creative work the legal right to exclusively use and distribute that work, often for a limited time	They copyrighted the book to avoid others from copying and reprinting it.

→ to define the duration

| to clarify the time during which something continues to be valid or exist | It is important to define the duration of Mr. Jinn's exclusive right to use the patent. |

→ to derive financial benefit

| to acquire a financial advantage from something | The author derived great financial benefit from copyrighting his new book. |

→ to disclose on a public register

| to make something known by listing it in a public database | Shares, Inc. disclosed its new trademark on the public register. |

→ to enforce rights (e.g. patent rights)

| to compel compliance with or observance of a right, e.g. the right to exclude others from selling a patented invention | The inventor enforced his patent rights against the company that was trying to copy his creation. |

→ to engage in cybersquatting

| to register names as internet domains in the hope of making a profit from reselling them in the future | Two university students engaged in cybersquatting and made a small fortune. |

→ to ensure intellectual property protection

| to safeguard creations and work from unfair competition through rights conferred by a patent, copyright, or trademark | The songwriter was quick to ensure intellectual property protection of his work. |

→ to expire automatically

| to lapse or cease to be valid as a result of certain laws | Mr. Jinn's right to the patent expired automatically after 20 years. |

→ to exploit the exclusive right

to take full and sole advantage, as a named licensee, of intellectual property rights	The author exploited his exclusive right to release the work to the media.

→ to file an application/trademark

to submit an official request to an authority, e.g. a patent application	Mr. Jinn filed an application for a patent to protect his new medical invention.

→ to grant exclusive rights/patent/copyright

to give someone a sole privilege or entitlement to have or do something	The court granted Mr. Jinn exclusive rights to the patent for a limited time of 20 years.

→ to have/hold rights in a creation

to have certain privileges or entitlements to a work, e.g. distribution, display, or reproduction	The inventor held rights in her unique car seat creation.

→ to infringe the rights

to breach or violate the rights of another person, e.g. to violate a person's rights under copyright, trademark, or patent	Ms. Hay infringed Mr. Jinn's patent rights.

→ to be inherently distinctive

to be entirely new and subject to trademark registration	KODAK is an inherently distinctive trademark.

→ to be liable for copyright infringement

to be guilty of using works protected by copyright law without permission or infringing certain exclusive rights belonging to the copyright holder	The author was liable for copyright infringement, as she adapted the original works of Ron Mowling without permission to do so.

→ to license the use of something

to permit the use or sale of intellectual property for a certain purpose, in return for compensation	The committee licensed the medication's use and sale in the form of a patent license to Mr. Jinn.

→ to object to the registration/filing of a trademark

to oppose the registration of a certain symbol, word, phrase, or design in a trademark database	The company objected to the registration of a pear symbol, claiming it infringed the company's trademark.

→ to own/license/reproduce work

to have the rights to use something in a particular way, which often includes the right to reproduce and share	He owned the rights to the song.

→ to patent an invention

to obtain an exclusive right to make, use, or sell an invention for a specified period of time (usually 20 years)	The inventor patented his revolutionary invention.

→ to prohibit copying of material

to disallow the reproduction or duplication of work	The author applied for a copyright to prohibit unauthorized copying of his book.

→ to prohibit or authorize reproduction/distribution/adaptation

to forbid or allow the copying of work/sharing of work/change to existing work	The artist prohibited unauthorized reproduction of his music.

→ to protect trade secrets

to institute special procedures for handling secret information, i.e. technological and security measures	Most beverage companies take steps to protect their trade secrets, including their recipes and any unique bottling techniques.

→ to be publicly available

| to be accessible to anyone who is interested | The information regarding the medication is now publicly available. |

→ to raise the potential for

| to increase the quality or ability of something, which may lead to future success | Patents usually have a maximum duration of twenty years to raise the potential for further inventions and discoveries. |

→ to register for copyright protection

| to submit a formal application for copyright of a work with the relevant copyright office | The author registered for copyright protection in his book. |

→ to renew a trademark

| to make a written request to keep a current trademark registration active before it expires | McGreer, Inc. renewed its green "McG" trademark. |

→ to seek/grant an injunction

| to request/award the judicial right to restrain another person from beginning or continuing an action that threatens or violates the legal right of another, or the right to compel a person to act | The author sought an injunction to stop Tom from printing and selling the author's work without permission. |

→ to trademark a symbol/phrase/logo

| to register a symbol, phrase, logo, or design as representing a company or product distinctively | After expanding for several years, the company decided to trademark the distinctive black and green symbol it used to distinguish itself from its competitors. |

9 Antitrust/Competition Law

A. Key Legal Terms

a. *Introduction*

• *antitrust law* • *competition law* • *in restraint of trade* • *anti-competitive*	*Antitrust law* (UK: *competition law*), which, in the US, consists of certain federal and state laws, is intended to regulate business practices which are *in restraint of trade* (UK: *anti-competitive*), with the goal of promoting fair competition among companies, and a resulting greater degree of choice for consumers.
• *competition authorities*	In the US, the Federal Trade Commission (FTC), the Department of Justice (DOJ), and private parties affected by commercial activities in restraint of trade can bring legal actions under antitrust law. In many other jurisdictions, *competition authorities* enforce the law.
• *Competition Act* • *Sherman Antitrust Act* • *Treaty on the Functioning of the European Union*	Various competition, antitrust, or cartel acts enable different countries' competition authorities to regulate competition. Some examples include the *UK's Competition Act of 1998,* the *US' Sherman Antitrust Act of 1890,* and Articles 101 and 102 of the *Treaty on the Functioning of the European Union* [TFEU], formerly Articles 81 and 82 of the Treaty establishing the European Community.

• *corporations* • *companies* • *enterprises* • *undertakings* • *firms* • *concerns* • *business entities*	Under EU competition law, examining the conduct of *corporations* (**UK:** *companies*) or other corporate *enterprises* (**UK:** *undertakings, firms, concerns, business entities*) requires identifying, on a case-by-case basis, the relevant geographic and product markets in which the corporate enterprises operate.

An *undertaking* (noun) in the TFEU refers to a company; to undertake to do something (verb) is to promise or commit oneself to do it, e.g. the Director of the undertaking undertook to abide by the agreed date.

b.   *Merger control*

• *monopoly* • *oligopoly*	Mergers between companies can lead to the creation of *monopolies* or *oligopolies*.
• *merger* • *acquisition* • *joint venture*	Under US law, collectively federal statutes known as the Clayton Act prohibit certain *mergers, acquisitions,* or *joint ventures* that may result in substantially lessened competition, or that tend to create a monopoly. Like competition authorities in other jurisdictions, the US FTC and DOJ review numerous merger filings annually.

The high-tech company merged with a competitor.

c.   *Monopoly and dominance*

• *dominant position*	A company has a *dominant position* if it can limit competition by making it difficult for another company to enter into and freely operate in the market.

• *abuse of monopoly power* • *barriers to entry* • *predatory pricing* • *price-fixing* • *tie-in arrangements*	Having a dominant position is not prohibited; abusing such a position is. Examples of the abuse of a dominant position (also *abuse of monopoly power*) include *barriers to entry* i.e. obstacles such as high start-up costs or excessive government regulations that make it difficult for a new company to enter into a given market; *predatory pricing* which refers to the very low pricing of products so as to eliminate competition; *price-fixing* or the setting of prices contrary to the free market workings of supply and demand; and *tie-in arrangements* which require consumers to purchase other (often unwanted) products produced by a company in order to keep the warranty valid.

Antitrust laws are designed to prevent the abuse of monopoly power.

d.   Cartels and collusion

• *cartel* • *collusion*	A *cartel* refers to a group of independent companies in similar sectors that agree to cooperate in order to limit competition (e.g. by controlling prices). *Collusion* is where companies (through their officers or other employees) seem to act independently while in fact conspiring to defraud or otherwise gain an unfair advantage over competitors, consumers, or suppliers with whom they are negotiating.
• *bid-rigging* • *collusive tendering*	*Bid-rigging* (also known as *collusive tendering*) is the practice of conspiring to fix a bid so that the lowest bidder gets the job.

• *vertical agreement* • *horizontal agreement*	Agreements between different players at different levels of the supply chain are *vertical agreements*, while an agreement among competitors to cooperate among themselves in providing goods or services to their customers is known as a *horizontal agreement*.
• *parallel behavior*	The practice of companies offering services at prices coordinated with their competitors is known as *parallel behavior*.

To bid for something is to offer to do it for a stated price (also to tender for). Usually, the lowest bidder is then awarded the contract.

e.   Sanctions/enforcement

• *leniency program/ leniency policy*	Corporate directors implicated in cartel activities or other activities in violation of antitrust law may face individual criminal prosecution under certain circumstances. However, under the DOJ's *leniency program* (UK/ EU: *leniency policy*), corporations and individuals who self-report their cartel activity voluntarily and choose to cooperate with the DOJ's investigation may face reduced sanctions or be able to avoid criminal conviction, fines, and incarceration altogether if they satisfy the program's criteria.
• *dawn raid* • *inspection without notice*	Under the competition laws of some EU countries, a *dawn raid* (also *inspection without notice*) is an unannounced visit by a law enforcement agency or the competition authorities to secure evidence and arrest persons suspected of violating competition law.

> The Department of Justice began its investigations after being approached by one of the cartel members offering evidence in the hopes of obtaining leniency.

f.   Call for tenders

• *Request for Proposals* • *request for bids*	A *Request for Proposals* (**RFP**) or *request for bids* is a special procedure for obtaining offers from different companies competing to secure a contract. It is essentially an invitation to potential bidders to submit a quote in response to precise specifications.

B.   Sample Definitions

bid rigging	Illegal bid rigging involves collusion among bidders, which undermines the bidding process and restricts competition, for example when competitors agree in advance who will win a bid.
dominant position	Situation in which the competitive pressure on one or more businesses is limited or non-existent, with the result that these businesses can limit competition by making it difficult for another company to enter into and freely operate in the market.
dawn raid	Unannounced search of business premises, private homes or vehicles by a law enforcement agency or certain EU competition authorities in order to find and secure evidence.

C.   Collocations Corner

→ to bid for something

| to make an offer of payment | Landt Inc. made a $20 billion bid for Norris Corporation. |

→ to drive down prices

| to force a price to go down | Competition among car dealers has driven down prices. |

→ to eliminate competition

| to completely remove competitors from the market | The company was able to eliminate competition from cheaper imports. |

→ to enter the market

| to become a part of a particular area of business or industry | Landt Inc. entered the retail market for chocolate. |

→ to erect barriers

| to create obstacles, e.g. high start up costs, restricting new competitors from easily entering an area of business | The company erected barriers to entry into the market to limit competition. |

→ to fix prices

| to secretly agree to set fixed prices for products together with other companies, rather than competing against each other | The judge fined five companies for fixing the price of aircraft parts sold in the United States. |

→ to gain an unfair advantage

| to produce an unfair advantage over competitors through deceptive trade practices | The company gained an unfair advantage over its competitors. |

→ to implement a decision

| to put a decision into effect or to carry out a decision | The trading company implemented the decision to take advantage of its competitor's trade mark. |

→ to impose a penalty

| to enforce a punishment | Courts may impose stiff penalties on companies that violate antitrust laws. |

→ to launch an inquiry (UK: enquiry)

| to conduct an investigation into a matter | The FTC launched an inquiry into the pharmaceutical sector. |

→ to limit competition

| to restrict competitive practices within a market | The company engaged in conduct in restraint of trade by colluding with others to limit competition in the computer chip technology market. |

→ to monitor a situation

| to observe and regulate the progress of a situation over a period of time | After monitoring the situation for some time, the FTC determined that the company was engaging in conduct in restraint of trade. |

→ to notify the authorities

| to inform an authority formally about something | He notified the relevant authorities of the situation. |

→ to obtain leniency

| to be granted immunity or reduced sanctions for cartel activity | The company director obtained leniency under the DOJ's leniency program. |

→ to promote competition

| to encourage and aid competition between corporations in an area of business | These laws promote competition and protect consumers from anti-competitive mergers. |

→ to regulate anti-competitive behavior

to enforce rules to control practices suppressing economic competition	The legislation sought to regulate anti-competitive behavior.

→ to rig a bid

to engage in illegal behavior that undermines the genuine bidding process, e.g. when competitors agree in advance who will win a bid for a business contract	The company was charged with rigging bids in the aircraft industry.

→ to secure a contract

to succeed in obtaining or to lock in a contract	The company secured a contract worth $10 million.

→ to submit a quote

to present an estimated cost for a particular service	The companies submitted their quotes for consideration.

Personal Notes _____

_____

_____

_____

_____

_____

_____

10 Civil Procedure

A. Key Legal Terms

a. *The court system*

federal courts *state courts*	In many jurisdictions, the law provides for three levels or tiers of courts. Some countries, including the US, also have two categories of courts, i.e. *federal courts* which have jurisdiction to hear certain matters, and *state courts*.
trial court *district court*	The first level is generally a *trial court* for a broad variety of claims, often called a *district court*. In the US, a federal district court will be identified as a United States District Court, as well as by its location and area of coverage, e.g. the United States District Court for the Southern District of New York, or the United States District Court for the Northern District of California.
appellate level *court of appeals* *appeals court*	The second, *appellate level* features a court of appeals (US state appellate court), e.g. the Colorado *Court of Appeals*, a Circuit Court (US federal appellate court), e.g. the United States Court of Appeals for the Third Circuit, or *appeals court* (UK).
supreme court	The highest court level is generally a *supreme court*. In the US, different states have their own state supreme courts, e.g. the Supreme Court of Pennsylvania, while the federal judicial system has a single supreme court, considered the highest court in the land, and known as the Supreme Court of the United States.
High Court	In non-US jurisdictions, the term *High Court* can refer to an appellate-level court or a supreme court, depending on the jurisdiction.

- *Tax Courts*
- *Labour Courts*
- *Landlord and Tenant Courts*
- *Bankruptcy Courts*
- *Small Claims Courts*

Note that some US states, most notably New York, employ a different nomenclature for their courts. In New York, the New York State Supreme Court is the trial court of general jurisdiction for civil cases. The Appellate Division of the New York State Supreme Court is the state's appellate-level court, while the Court of Appeals is New York's highest state court. Different jurisdictions may also have specialized courts, e.g. *Tax Courts* (US), *Labour Courts* (UK), *Landlord and Tenant Courts* (UK), *Bankruptcy Courts* (US), and *Small Claims Courts* (US).

- *venue*
- *personal jurisdiction*
- *territorial jurisdiction*
- *subject-matter jurisdiction*

Whether a court has jurisdiction to hear cases concerning events or persons within a particular geographic area depends on whether *venue* is proper and whether the court has *personal jurisdiction* over the defendant. The concept of personal jurisdiction in the US is related to the concept of *territorial jurisdiction*. *Subject-matter jurisdiction* refers to a court's power to hear cases relating to a specific subject matter. Tax Courts, for example, have the authority to hear tax law cases only.

The *court* refused to hear the case on the grounds that it lacked *jurisdiction*.

10

b.   *The parties*

• *plaintiff* • *claimant* • *defendant* • *appellant* • *petitioner* • *appellee* • *respondent*	The *plaintiff* (UK: *claimant*) is the party initiating legal proceedings by filing a complaint against the *defendant*. In appellate cases, the party appealing a lower court's decision is known as the *appellant* or *petitioner*, while the other party is known as the *appellee* or *respondent*. An appellee may also cross-appeal a portion or all of the lower court's decision.
• *litigant*	Parties to a lawsuit are referred to as *litigants*. Plaintiffs and defendants are both litigants.

NB These terms apply to court procedure in civil cases only. Criminal cases, hearings before tribunals, and other means of dispute resolution may use different terms that may also vary from jurisdiction to jurisdiction.

c.   *Legal counsel*

• *attorney* • *attorney-at-law* • *solicitor* • *barrister* • *right of audience* • *in-house counsel* • *outside counsel*	An *attorney* may be either an agent or legal representative authorized to act on someone else's behalf. In the US, an *attorney-at-law* is trained and licensed to practice law. In many common law jurisdictions apart from the US, the legal profession is split between *solicitors* and *barristers* (the latter of whom may also be referred to as counsel, legal counsel, counsel for the defense, or counsel for the prosecution) where only barristers have the *right of audience* in higher courts. *In-house counsel* (as opposed to *outside counsel*) are fully qualified legal professionals employed by a business or government department.

• *lawyer* • *legal trainee*	The generic term *lawyer* generally refers to a person licensed to practice law. In some jurisdictions, a *legal trainee* is a law graduate undergoing professional training at a law firm (or government authority) to qualify as a full-fledged lawyer.

After graduating from law school and passing the bar exam, she was able to practice as an attorney.

d.   *The documents*

• *complaint* • *summons*	The document which sets out the plaintiff's allegations and claims is the *complaint*. Proceedings in the US commence when the plaintiff files a complaint with the court, and then serves the complaint, along with a *summons*, upon the defendant.
• *answer* • *counterclaim* • *reply* • *causes of action*	The defendant responds with an *answer*, and may also file a *counterclaim* against the plaintiff. The plaintiff can respond to the answer by means of a *reply*. The legal claims made in these documents are the *causes of action*, i.e. the legal reason(s) for taking legal action such as breach of contract, tort, or violation of a right.
• *default judgment*	If the defendant fails to answer the complaint or to appear before the court, the court may render a *default judgment*.

• *brief*	When a party to a legal proceeding files a motion requesting that the court take action on a particular matter (e.g. a motion to transfer venue, a motion to extend a deadline, a motion to reschedule a hearing, a motion to exclude evidence, a motion to dismiss, or a motion for summary judgment), the motion often includes a separate document called a *brief,* which sets forth the relevant facts, law, and legal arguments. In the UK, the term brief also refers to the papers a barrister receives when instructed by a solicitor.
• *pleadings* • *struck*	Collectively, the formal written statements filed with a court by parties to initiate a civil action are referred to as the *pleadings*. Pleadings not accepted by the court may be *struck*.

After filing the *complaint*, the plaintiff must serve the complaint and a *summons* on the defendant.

e.   *Court procedure*

• *mediation*	Some jurisdictions require that the parties, before filing a claim, engage in an attempt at conciliation before a designated *mediation* authority.
• *ordinary proceedings* • *simplified proceedings*	All disputes which are not governed by special proceedings are governed by *ordinary proceedings*. In some jurisdictions *simplified proceedings* may be appropriate for cases with an amount in dispute of up to $30,000, as well as for specialized matters such as landlord/tenant, employment, and consumer disputes.

• *motion* • *ruling* • *order* • *stay in proceedings* • *stay*	In common law jurisdictions, *a motion* is a written or oral application made to a court to obtain a ruling or order in favor of the applicant. It may be used to resolve a dispute without the need for a full hearing. The court responds by issuing a *ruling* or *order* setting out its finding, e.g. calling a temporary halt to the case (known as a *stay in proceedings*), or dismissing the case for want of evidence. A *stay* may also be agreed upon to allow the parties to settle.
• *ex parte hearing*	In urgent cases, a court can hear a matter *ex parte*, i.e. without hearing the opposing party.
• *class action*	*Class action* lawsuits are unique to the US, although a new UK law permits one or more individuals to bring a consumer rights action on behalf of a much larger group.
• *decision* • *ruling* • *finding*	Having completed its deliberations, the court will render its *decision* (also referred to as a *ruling* or *finding*).
• *appeal* • *affirm* • *reverse* • *remand*	In many common law jurisdictions, parties may *appeal* a lower court's decision, but may not always have an automatic right to appellate review. An appeals court can *affirm* or *reverse* the order or decision of a lower court, or *remand* the case, i.e. send it back to the lower court for further action.
• *enforcement procedures*	*Enforcement procedures* compel compliance with court orders.

Lawyers can file *motions*; judges may grant or deny them.
Parties appear before court; the court hears their case.

f.   Collecting evidence

10

• *discovery* • *disclosure*	In common law jurisdictions, once a lawsuit has been filed, and prior to trial, each party can obtain evidence from the opposing party (US: *discovery*; UK: *disclosure*); however, the scope of documents to be disclosed in the UK is more limited than in the US discovery phase.
• *demand for particulars* • *witness statements* • *affidavit* • *subpoena* • *depositions* • *interrogatories*	In the UK both parties to a suit can request further information (*demand for particulars*) which may include *witness statements* (formal documents containing the witnesses' accounts of the facts relating to the issue(s) arising in the dispute), and *affidavits* (similar in content to a witness statement but made under oath and notarized). A witness served with a witness summons is said to have been *subpoenaed*. *Depositions* and *interrogatories* are US terms referring to pretrial out-of-court witness testimony. A *deposition* involves questioning of a party or non-party witness by each party's lawyers. The witness provides oral responses, which are recorded in a deposition transcript and may but do not have to be videotaped. *Interrogatories* are formal written questions requesting information from a party or non-party witness, which the witness has a legal duty to answer truthfully and in full to the extent the interrogatories request information relevant to a matter.

• *witness testimony* • *expert opinions* • *documentary evidence*	The Anglo-American distinction between the pre-trial and trial phases is unknown in many civil law jurisdictions, where a "trial" consists of an on-going succession of meetings, hearings, and written communications. In such jurisdictions, the judge supervises and cooperates in gathering evidence, including questioning witnesses directly. Admissible evidence may include *witness testimony, expert opinions, documentary evidence*, physical objects, and the questioning of the parties. The weight each piece of evidence receives is a matter of judicial discretion.

Counsel for the defendant filed a motion to dismiss the case on the grounds that the statute of limitations had expired, and that the plaintiff's allegations as stated in the complaint, even if found to be true, failed to state a claim for relief.

g.   *Legal remedies*

• *prayer for relief* • *request for relief*	The part of the complaint which describes the remedies the plaintiff seeks from the court is referred to as the *prayer for relief* (also *request for relief*).
• *damages* • *equitable remedies* • *specific performance* • *injunction*	If the court finds in favor of the plaintiff (or if the defendant's counterclaim is successful), it may award *damages* (the legal term for monetary compensation). If damages are not an adequate remedy, the court may grant an *equitable remedy* (UK and US) such as *specific performance*, or an *injunction* requiring the party enjoined to do or refrain from doing something.

| • *declaratory judgment*
 • *to find in favor*
 • *costs* | A court decision informing the parties of their rights and responsibilities (without awarding damages) is known as a *declaratory judgment*. Based on the facts and legal arguments presented, a court will *find in favor of* either the plaintiff or the defendant. The successful party to litigation may seek an order from the court that the unsuccessful party pay the successful party's *costs*. |

The court *found in favor* of the plaintiff and awarded *damages* in the amount of $10,000 plus interest and costs.

B.   Sample Definitions

injunction	Court order that requires a party to do or refrain from doing a certain act.
discovery	Procedure under US law in which the parties to a lawsuit are required to disclose information to each other, for example by handing over documents, giving depositions, and responding to interrogatories (written lists of questions).

C.   Collocations Corner

→ **to admit allegations**	
to acknowledge or confess that certain facts are true	He was instructed to admit the allegations and request time to pay the plaintiff.

→ **to agree to a stay**	
to consent to a court order temporarily suspending a proceeding	The parties agreed to a stay to secure the claimant's rights.

→ to grant or deny a motion to

to permit/refuse a request by a party for a particular ruling by the court	The judge denied the motion to exclude certain evidence.

→ to bar an action

to prevent a lawsuit from taking place	The judge barred an action for negligence, as the statute of limitations had expired.

→ to enforce a judgment

to impose a formal court decision	The creditor enforced a judgment against the debtor.

→ to file a claim

to submit a document (a legal assertion or demand) to the court requesting redress or compensation	Mr. Jones filed a claim against his employer.

→ to file with an authority

to submit an official document to an organization possessing administrative power	They filed their complaint with the Department of Justice.

→ to give evidence

to provide information and answer questions truthfully and formally in a court of law or during discovery	The witness gave evidence against the defendant.

→ to hear an argument

to listen critically to the reasons for or against a decision on a particular matter	The jury heard the plaintiff's argument on the breach of contract claim.

→ to initiate a claim

| to commence legal action by submitting a formal demand or assertion | He initiated a claim against his former employer. |

→ to lodge an appeal with (UK)

| to request review of a decision by a higher court | The lawyer lodged an appeal against the sentence. |

→ to obtain evidence

| to acquire facts or information that prove whether a belief or contention is true | The lawyers obtained evidence against the defendant. |

→ to raise a defense

| to put forth arguments and reasoning against a claim or charge in an attempt to avoid criminal or civil liability | He raised the defense of improper venue. |

→ to reach a decision

| to make a decision | The jury finally reached a decision after two days of deliberation. |

→ to rebut an argument

| to present evidence or facts that weaken an opponent's claim | Mr. Hall rebutted the argument that his client was drunk at the time. |

→ to seek leave to appeal

| to request permission from the court to appeal a decision | The barrister sought leave to appeal to the High Court (UK). |

→ to serve a summons on someone

| to legally bring court documents to a party's attention | Mr. Jones served a summons on the defendant. |

10

→ to submit a document

| to present documents for consideration | The panel submitted their report to the relevant committee. |

→ to testify for/against someone

| to make a statement based on personal experience or knowledge, usually as a witness in court, supporting or incriminating a party | Several witnesses testified against George. |

→ to weigh evidence

| to evaluate the credibility of evidence to reach a decision | The jury carefully weighed the evidence put forward by both parties. |

Personal Notes _____

_____

_____

_____

_____

_____

_____

_____

11 Arbitration

11

A.   Key Legal Terms

a.   Sources of law

• *international convention*	In international commercial arbitration the most important *international convention* is the 1958 New York Convention on Recognition and Enforcement of Foreign Arbitral Awards (New York Convention), whose principal aim is to ease the enforcement of foreign arbitral awards.
• *legislation* • *seat of arbitration*	Participation in arbitration is a matter of consent between the parties. Nevertheless, various countries have enacted *legislation* governing international arbitration. Such legislation typically applies if the *seat of arbitration* is in the country at issue, and at least one party was not domiciled in that country upon entering into the arbitration agreement.
• *lex arbitri*	*Lex arbitri* refers to the procedural law on arbitration of the country in which the arbitration takes place.

National *legislation* has a significant bearing on arbitral proceedings, as the proceedings are often governed by that legislation.

b.   *General terms*

• *arbitration*
 • *dispute resolution*
 • *arbitration/arbitral*
    tribunal
 • *sole arbitrator*
 • *arbitrator*
 • *party-appointed*
    arbitrator
 • *chairperson*
 • *challenge*
 • *arbitration*
    agreement/clause
	Arbitration is a method of *dispute resolution* often resorted to in disputes arising out of international commercial transactions. An *arbitration* (or *arbitral*) *tribunal* is a neutral body composed of a *sole arbitrator* or two or more *arbitrators*. Where the tribunal is composed of, for example, three arbitrators, the parties typically select one arbitrator each. The two *party-appointed arbitrators* choose the third arbitrator who acts as the *chairperson*. The parties' *arbitration agreement or arbitration clause* in the contract between them sets out the rules to be followed, e.g. the Rules of Arbitration of the International Chamber of Commerce (ICC Rules), or a particular jurisdiction's rules of international arbitration.

• *ad hoc arbitration*
 • *UNCITRAL*
    Arbitration Rules
 • *arbitration/arbitral*
    award
 • *determination on*
    the merits
 • *arbitrable*
 • *arbitrability*
 • *arbitral jurisdiction*
	Ad hoc arbitration is arbitration which is not administered by an arbitral institution such as the ICC. The *UNCITRAL Arbitration Rules* are commonly used in ad hoc arbitrations.
	
	 An *arbitration* (or *arbitral*) *award* is a *determination on the merits* of a case by an arbitration tribunal. It is similar to a judgment in a court of law.
	
	 An *arbitrable* dispute is one which may be submitted to arbitration. The question of *arbitrability* also determines *arbitral jurisdiction*.

The parties expressly acknowledged the jurisdiction of the arbitral tribunal and the choice of substantive New York federal law.

c.   *Procedure*

11

• *claimant* • *respondent* • *Request for Arbitration* • *Answer to Request for Arbitration* • *Terms of Reference* • *Redfern Schedule*	The parties to an arbitration are generally referred to as the *claimant* and the *respondent*. The claimant may initiate arbitration proceedings by submitting a *Request for Arbitration*. The respondent responds with an *Answer to Request for Arbitration*. The arbitral tribunal may, in cooperation with the parties, set out in the *Terms of Reference* the issues in dispute, the applicable rules, and the procedural timetable. To manage all the documentary evidence (and hence reduce the associated time and costs), parties may agree to adopt a so-called *Redfern Schedule*.
• *Statement of Claim* • *Requests and Pleas/ Prayers for Relief* • *Pleas for Relief* • *Statement of Defense* • *Statement of Counterclaim* • *dismiss with prejudice*	The claimant's case is set out in a *Statement of Claim*. The legal remedies – such as damages and the costs, fees, and disbursements of the arbitration – are sought by way of *Requests and Pleas* (or *Prayers*) *for Relief*. The respondent may respond with a *Statement of Defense* and also file a *Statement of Counterclaim*. Alternatively, the respondent may plead that the tribunal *dismiss* the claim *with prejudice*. If successful, the opposing party is than barred from having the same claim heard again.
• *procedural motions*	Should procedural questions arise in the course of the proceedings, either party may submit *procedural motions*.
• *set aside* • *challenge*	In many jurisdictions, the scope for challenging an international arbitration award is very limited. An award may be *set aside* if a party's right to be heard was violated, or it may be *challenged* if there was some serious irregularity on the part of the tribunal, or if the tribunal lacked jurisdiction. Arbitrators may also be the subject of a challenge, e.g. on the grounds of justifiable doubts about their independence.

The *respondent* submitted the *Statement of Defense* including the *Plea for Relief* that the claim be *dismissed with prejudice*.

B.   Sample Definitions

• *lex arbitri*	Law at the location of the arbitration tribunal, which governs the arbitration procedure.
• *arbitration*	Dispute resolution procedure carried out in a non-judicial venue known as an arbitration tribunal.
• *terms of reference*	Terms of reference contain a declaration by the parties that the arbitration tribunal has jurisdiction to resolve the dispute, and set out the parties' requests and pleas, the issues in dispute, the applicable law, and the procedural rules.

C.   Collocations Corner

→ to agree to arbitration	
to consent to alternative dispute resolution to avoid litigation and resolve a legal issue outside of court	The parties agreed to arbitration to maintain confidentiality regarding the matter.

→ to be entitled to recover costs	
to have the right as a successful party in legal proceedings to receive payment from the losing party to cover legal expenses	The court determined that Mr. Hall was not entitled to recover costs.

→ to challenge an award

| to dispute a determination, usually because of a tribunal's lack of jurisdiction or serious irregularity | I challenged the award on the grounds of bias. |

→ to enforce an award

| to compel parties to observe an arbitral determination | The court enforced the arbitrator's award. |

→ to go to arbitration

| to pursue alternative dispute resolution and have an arbitrator, rather than a judge, hear a case | The parties agreed to go to arbitration over the breached contract. |

→ to impose a decision

| to establish a binding resolution | The arbitrator imposed a decision on the parties. |

→ to initiate arbitration

| to commence arbitration by submitting a formal request to an arbitration institute | Mr. Smith initiated arbitration proceedings by giving notice to the other party. |

→ to present arguments

| to put forth reasoning and rationales for consideration and scrutiny | The parties presented their arguments and evidence to an arbitrator. |

→ to present evidence

| to put forth facts and information that indicate truth or validity | Ms. Smith presented evidence to the arbitral tribunal. |

→ to refer a matter to arbitration

to pass a legal matter on to an arbitrator or an arbitral tribunal to make a binding decision	The contract enabled the parties to refer the matter to arbitration.

→ to resolve a dispute

to render a formal decision on an issue or disagreement	The parties turned to arbitration to resolve their dispute in a more efficient manner.

→ to resort to arbitration

to adopt alternative dispute resolution to resolve a legal matter outside of court	The company resorted to arbitration after numerous failed attempts at reaching a settlement agreement.

→ to set aside an award

to render a determination void	The claimant sought to set aside the award on the basis that its right to be heard was violated.

→ to submit a matter to arbitration

to refer an issue in dispute to an arbitrator or an arbitral tribunal for resolution	The parties intended to submit the matter to arbitration.

→ to submit a motion

to file a request to obtain a ruling or decision from a judge	They submitted a motion to dismiss due to successful settlement.

→ to submit to arbitration

to agree to be bound by and comply with the decision of the arbitral tribunal	They submitted their disagreements to arbitration.

12 Bankruptcy Law

A.   Key Legal Terms

a.   *Introduction*

• *insolvency* • *debtor* • *in default* • *bankruptcy*	*Insolvency* is the inability of a person or a company to pay debts when they become due. The *debtor* is then known as being in *default*. *Bankruptcy* is a judicially regulated procedure by which the assets of a debtor are sold, and the money raised is distributed among the creditors in order of priority.
• *insolvent liquidation*	In the US, the term bankruptcy is used with respect to companies and individuals. In the UK, the term bankruptcy refers only to individuals. By contrast, UK companies face *insolvent liquidation*.
• *seizure* • *assets* • *liquidate* • *creditors* • *to extinguish obligations* • *the proceeds*	In the course of bankruptcy or insolvent liquidation proceedings, the courts or other authorities may issue an order requiring the seizure of a debtor's assets. The assets may then be *liquidated* to meet the debtor's obligations to *creditors*, thus *extinguishing* these pre-bankruptcy or pre-insolvency *obligations*. Assets liquidated in this way are often referred to as *the proceeds*.

12

- *over-indebtedness*
- *insolvent*
- *realize assets*
- *discharge debts*
- *debt restructuring agreement*
- *deed of arrangement*
- *to stay*
- *file for protection*
- *Chapter 11*

When a company faces *over-indebtedness* (i.e. is unable to meet its financial obligations on time) or becomes *insolvent*, it must take steps to remedy the situation, e.g. borrow more money to finance those debts; *realize its assets* to *discharge its debts*; renegotiate the debt (e.g. for lower interest rates); enter into a *debt restructuring agreement* (UK: Company Voluntary Agreement (CVA) or *deed of arrangement*); or notify the appropriate court. The court will commence insolvency proceedings and may appoint an administrative receiver to, inter alia, dispose of the company's assets. In many jurisdictions, bankruptcy or other formal insolvency proceedings may be *stayed* if the debts are settled or a settlement agreement can be reached with the creditors. Debt restructuring agreements are judicially supervised or out-of-court settlements between debtors and their creditor(s) to avoid full bankruptcy/insolvency proceedings (in the US companies may *file for protection* under *Chapter 11*).

- *solvent*
- *voluntary liquidation*
- *fiduciary duty*

If a company is in financial difficulties though still *solvent*, the shareholders may agree to put the company into *voluntary liquidation*. The directors of an insolvent company owe their *fiduciary duty* to the creditors.

Insolvency describes the financial status of a company; *bankruptcy* (UK: *insolvent liquidation*) the judicial procedure to address creditors' claims.

In September 2008 the financial services firm Lehman Brothers *filed for Chapter 11 bankruptcy protection*. It was the largest bankruptcy filing in US history.

b.   *Introductory proceedings*

• *debt collection request* • *debt collection office*	Creditors may generally initiate debt enforcement proceedings by filing a *debt collection request* against the debtor with the appropriate *debt collection office*. The debt agency then serves a summons for payment on the debtor. At this stage the creditor does not yet have to prove the validity of the claim. If the debtor fails to respond, the proceedings will continue for the amount claimed by the creditor. If debtors wish to contest a creditor's claim, they may submit a written or verbal objection to the debt collection agency. In order to proceed with the enforcement of the claim, the creditor must then obtain from the appropriate court an order dismissing the objection.
• *bankruptcy petitions* • *default judgment* • *bankruptcy order*	In the UK, *bankruptcy petitions* are usually presented at a court with bankruptcy jurisdiction closest to where the debtor lives or trades. If the debtor fails to respond the court can enter a *default judgment*. If the matter is contested and the court finds for the creditor, it will issue a *bankruptcy order.*
• *joint and several liability*	In a partnership, all partners are usually *jointly and severally liable* to the full extent of their assets; hence, if one partner goes bankrupt, creditors can claim the whole amount from the remaining partner(s).

As the defendant did not respond to the summons for payment, the court entered judgment against him.

c.   Remedies

- *secured*
- *unsecured*
- *preferential*
- *favored status*
- *lien*
- *priority*
- *security*
- *first-in-time rules*

Creditors may be *secured, unsecured,* or *preferential.* Where debtors fail to honor their debts when due, and creditors initiate proceedings against them to enforce their claims, creditors with *favored status* are more likely to have their debts satisfied first. This favored status might have been acquired by *lien* or by *priority.* A lien is a right to retain possession of another's property as *security* or payment for a debt; priority is calculated by *first-in-time rules* or according to the class of creditor.

- *mortgage*
- *security interests*
- *collateral*
- *consensual liens*
- *perfection*

A *mortgage* is a lien created over land, while *security interests* generally relate to interests in other types of property (then often referred to as *collateral*). A lien such as a mortgage is known as a *consensual lien* because it has been agreed to by the debtor and the creditor. A consensual lien can only be invoked against third parties (e.g. other creditors with interests in the same property) when it has been *perfected*, for example by registration.

- *judicial liens*
- *bailiff*
- *garnishment*
- *attachment*

Liens arising out of judicial proceedings brought by a creditor to secure an interest in the debtor's property are referred to as *judicial liens*. Such liens usually empower a *bailiff* – a court-appointed public official – to seize the debtor's property to enforce his obligations. *Garnishment*, for example, is a court order to a third party who owes money to the debtor (such as the debtor's employer) to release that money to the creditor. The concept of *attachment* is similar to garnishment. If a court, upon motion, issues a writ of attachment, the sheriff may seize ("attach") the property specified in the writ and hold it in his custody until the court issues a judgment in the underlying case.

• *statutory liens* • *tax liens*	*Statutory liens,* such as *tax liens* securing payment to the government for outstanding taxes, are liens created by statute.
• *attachment lien* • *attachment order* • *distraint order* • *freezing order* • *Mareva injunction*	A court order to seize a debtor's property after the creditor has initiated judicial proceedings against a debtor but before a decision has been reached is known as an *attachment lien* or an *attachment order.* Such a lien (**UK**: *freezing order, Mareva injunction*) operates to seize the debtor's assets provisionally to prevent their transfer or disposal by the debtor.
• *judgment lien*	If the court decides in the claimant's favor, a *judgment lien* may apply. This attaches to the debtor's assets immediately.
• *winding up order* • *involuntary bankruptcy*	For companies, either the creditor(s) or the company directors may petition the court for a *winding up order,* whereupon the company is put into *involuntary bankruptcy.*
• *foreclosure* • *mortgage* • *pledged property*	In order to satisfy a debt, the creditor may initiate debt enforcement proceedings to *foreclose* the lien (for example on a *mortgage* or other *pledged property*) and have the property sold.
• *called in* • *stay*	Failure to duly repay a loan may result in the debtor being deemed to be in default and the balance *called in,* i.e. immediate payment demanded. In many jurisdictions, the debtor may *stay* the debt enforcement proceedings if the debts are settled, or if the debtor and creditors enter into a settlement agreement.

The bank chose to enforce its security in the property by applying to the court for a *foreclosure* order.

d.   Asset protection

- *asset protection plans*
- *contempt of court*
- *bankruptcy fraud*
- *fraudulent conveyance*

Asset protection plans are designed to limit a potential debtor's exposure in the event of indebtedness because assets properly protected cannot be reached by creditors. However, debtors may face charges of *contempt of court* or *bankruptcy fraud* should they fail to fully disclose the entirety of their assets and asset transfers. The transfer of property for the express purpose of putting it beyond the reach of a known creditor may be a *fraudulent conveyance* and can be set aside by the court at the request of the defrauded creditor.

Debtors who conceal assets in order to avoid having to forfeit them (forced to give them up) risk criminal proceedings.

e.   Insolvency professionals

- *receiver*
- *in receivership*
- *official receiver*

A *receiver* acts on behalf of a creditor to manage a company in such a way as to recover monies owed. Such a company is said to be *in receivership* and ceases its activities. In some jurisdictions an *official receiver* is an officer of the court responsible for administering a debtor's bankruptcy and protecting the debtor's assets from the date of the bankruptcy order.

• *administrator*	By contrast, an *administrator* is a court-appointed
• *in administration*	official who takes over a company in financial
• *liquidator*	difficulties to maintain it as a going concern, i.e.
• *wind up*	to keep it operating in the interests of all parties
• *realize assets*	including the employees. Such a company is
• *insolvency*	said to be *in administration*. A *liquidator* is a person
practitioner	appointed by the shareholders or unsecured
• *bankruptcy trustee*	creditors or the court to *wind up* or *realize the assets*
• *trustee in*	of a company to settle the claims against it. A
bankruptcy	liquidator may also be known as an *insolvency*
	practitioner (**UK**), *bankruptcy trustee*, or *trustee in*
	bankruptcy (**US**). Insolvency practitioners can
	also advise clients on insolvency and bankrupt-
	cy proceedings.

When the company was *declared insolvent* a *liquidator* was appointed to *wind up* its affairs.

f.   Jurisdiction in bankruptcy

• *recognition*	In general, the law applicable to bankruptcy
• *reciprocity*	proceedings is that of the state where the
• *decree*	insolvency proceedings commence. The
	appropriate court is the one where the debtor's
	main interests are located. In some jurisdictions,
	a foreign bankruptcy has no effect unless a
	court or other tribunal of the jurisdiction at
	issue has *recognized* the bankruptcy (based on,
	inter alia, *reciprocity*), following which the foreign
	bankruptcy order (or *decree*) relating to the
	debtor's assets located in the jurisdiction has
	the same effect as a domestic bankruptcy order.

A court may have to decide whether or not to recognize a foreign court's order in bankruptcy proceedings.

B.   Sample Definitions

debt enforcement proceedings	Debt enforcement proceedings may involve the seizure of assets, the enforcement of secured claims, or bankruptcy, whereby the debtor's assets may be seized and liquidated by the authorities, but only to the extent required to meet the creditors' claims.
debt enforcement request	Written or oral application by a creditor to a debt enforcement office requesting that debt enforcement proceedings be taken against a debtor. It normally contains the particulars of the creditor and debtor, details of the amount of the debt, and, if possible, documentary evidence of the debt.
garnishment	Temporary seizure of earnings in possession of a third party in order to secure the creditor's claim.
liquidator	Person appointed by the shareholders or the court to wind up or realize the assets of a company in order to settle the claims against it.

C. Collocations Corner

→ to be in arrears

to owe money that should have already been paid	They were two months in arrears on their mortgage.

→ to be in default

to fail to meet legal obligations (e.g. interest payments of a loan/debt)	She was in default after failing to pay her student loan for 280 days.

→ to call in a loan

to request repayment of a loan immediately or within a short period	Given Mr. Hall's financial instability, the bank called in his loan of $1,000,000.

→ to declare bankruptcy

to make an application to the court admitting inability to pay debts and asking for a discharge of those debts	He had no option but to declare bankruptcy on Friday.

→ to discharge one's debts

to relieve a borrower from obligations to a lender	Once its debts were discharged, the company began operating again.

→ to enforce a debt

to take action to recover debts, e.g. through seizing assets, enforcing secured claims, or filing for bankruptcy	The bank may enforce a debt against a borrower upon the borrower's failure to pay his mortgage interest.

→ to enter judgment against

to enter an order that enables a creditor to take action to recover unpaid debts, e.g. through seizing assets, enforcing secured claims, or filing for bankruptcy	To enter a judgment against a borrower, the creditor must take the borrower to court.

→ to file for protection

to request a formal, legal schedule allowing the debtor to create a plan to pay debts and present the plan to creditors	The company filed for protection from its creditors.

→ to foreclose on a property

to attempt to recover the balance of a loan from a borrower by forcing sale of the asset used as security for the loan	The bank has just informed me of its plans to foreclose on my home.

→ to go bankrupt

to be unable to pay debts and thereby to become subject to the legal procedure of selling assets to raise money for creditors	The company went bankrupt.

→ to liquidate assets

to divide a company's assets among creditors and shareholders in order of priority, following a company's insolvency	The bank has commenced liquidating the assets of ABC Financial Corporation.

→ to obtain/procure a court order

to acquire a court order that requires a party to take a certain action, e.g. paying a sum of money	The bank obtained/procured a court order against Mr. Smith, requiring that he repay his debts to all his creditors.

→ to open bankruptcy proceedings

to initiate a court action for relief from debts by making court-approved plans for partial repayment	The creditors opened involuntary bankruptcy proceedings against the debtor.

→ to realize assets

to sell assets to generate income	The liquidator will realize the company's assets to pay off the creditors.

→ to recover losses

to regain outstanding debts from the bankrupt individual or corporate entity in part or in full	The bank hopes to recover the majority of its losses resulting from the unpaid mortgage.

→ to satisfy a debt

to repay an outstanding amount	This asset must be used to satisfy the debt to the creditor.

→ to secure a debt

to guarantee that the borrower can satisfy a debt by offering an asset (often a property or shares) as collateral	His debt was secured by a mortgage on his house.

→ to seize assets

to confiscate a debtor's assets legally to secure a creditor's claim	The bankruptcy administrator determined that the court could seize the debtor's assets to satisfy his outstanding loans.

→ to service a debt

to repay interest and principal on a debt over a period of time (e.g. mortgage interest payments)	Unable to service its debts, the company went insolvent.

→ to settle one's debts

to negotiate with creditors to reduce overall debts	You might be able to settle your credit card debts for less than you owe.

→ to stay proceedings

to suspend a civil procedure in court on bankruptcy grounds	The court granted a stay of proceedings because the corporate defendant had initiated bankruptcy proceedings.

→ to take out a loan

to borrow a sum of money that is expected to be paid back with interest	Mary took out a loan to buy the car of her dreams.

→ to take/initiate remedial action

to take action in response to breached obligations (e.g. non-payment of a loan) to correct an existing issue or prevent further issues from arising	Creditors may take remedial action against the debtor with respect to his property.

→ to wind up a company

to bring a corporate entity to an end by selling all of its assets to pay off creditors	Winding up ABC Ltd may take up to three years.

Personal Notes _____

_____

_____

_____

_____

_____

_____

_____

13 Tax Law

A.   Key Legal Terms

a.   *Types of taxation*

• *income tax* • *resident* • *domiciled* • *corporate tax* • *permanent establishment*	Tax law introduces a liability to pay tax which is imposed by the relevant tax-raising authority upon individuals and organizations. Generally speaking, individuals are liable for *income tax* if they are *resident* or *domiciled* in the jurisdiction of the tax authority in question. For international companies, the test for liability for *corporate tax* will always be more complex. It depends on a range of issues, such as whether the entity has a *permanent establishment* in the jurisdiction.
• *capital gains tax* • *realized gain* • *inheritance tax* • *estate tax*	*Capital gains tax* is determined by assessing the *realized gains* arising from the disposal of defined assets such as real estate or stock market securities. *Inheritance tax* (imposed on heirs in some jurisdictions) and *estate tax* (imposed on the decedent's estate in the US), are taxes imposed on transfers that occur upon death (and, in some jurisdictions, as a donation retrospectively on certain lifetime transfers within a defined period before the decedent's death).

• *value added tax* • *sales tax* • *stamp duty* • *withholding tax*	*Value added tax* or *sales tax* (US) are consumption taxes applied on a wide range of goods sold or services rendered in the course of business. *Stamp duty* (UK) is the tax collected for stamping legal documents in order to give the transaction – such as the purchase of land – legal effect. *Withholding tax* is an amount that must be deducted by the payer (usually a bank) before distributing amounts such as dividends or interest to the recipient.
• *federal* • *state* • *municipal*	In many countries, the tax system allows taxes to be levied on three levels: *federal*, *state*, and *municipal*. Tax burdens can vary considerably depending on the respective state and municipal tax regimes. Consequently, detailed tax planning (including the location of the business and other factors relating to taxation) is essential.

The UK has introduced a tax known as the "non-dom" charge. It is a set amount of tax to be paid each year if one has been resident but not domiciled in the UK for over seven years.

b.   *Basis of taxation in law*

• *deduction at source* • *tax rate*	For individuals, income tax is sometimes, and only in some jurisdictions, payable through a process of *deduction at source* (which is also called PAYE [in the UK] or "pay as you earn"), and follows a *tax rate which* depends on an individual's net tax liability after certain allowances and deductions.

- *declaration*
- *deductible expenses*
- *tax return*
- *assessment*
- *tax tribunal*

VAT or sales tax is also a tax that is collected at source by, for example, adding the tax to the cost of the product or service. Alternatively, taxpayers make a *declaration* of their earnings less *deductible expenses* in a *tax return,* and in some jurisdictions, this is then followed by an *assessment* of the tax liability by the tax authority. If the assessment is accepted, taxpayers must pay their taxes within the requisite time period. Failure to do so results in penalties and interest charges. Different jurisdictions provide for different types of appeals in case a taxpayer disputes the tax authority's determination of the taxpayer's liability. In the US, taxpayers have the right to have a challenge to a decision by the taxing authority reviewed by an IRS Office of Appeals other than the IRS office which initially rendered the decision. Alternatively, taxpayers who have objected to the position of the IRS and who have received a statutory notice of deficiency may petition the US Tax Court for review prior to paying the tax.

Resident companies and foreign companies' permanent establishments are usually subject to income taxes and capital gains taxes. Criteria for determining whether a company is resident include the registered seat of the company or the effective place of directive management.

- *foreign tax credits*

Income can be taxed at the company and shareholder level. Taxes paid in one jurisdiction can themselves constitute tax-deductible items for tax assessments in another jurisdiction (so called *foreign tax credits*).

13

| • *double taxation treaties* | *Double taxation treaties* have been agreed between countries to either reduce or avoid multiple tax charges where the same item of income is liable to taxation in more than one jurisdiction. There are mechanisms in place to allow double taxation relief either by declaring that income is exempt in one of the tax jurisdictions, or by providing a credit against local tax for foreign tax already paid. |

The head office of the principal company used to be readily identifiable, but this is not always the case for true multinationals.

The taxpayer contested the decision that he owed back taxes despite the *double taxation treaty*.

Personal Notes _____

_____

_____

_____

_____

_____

_____

I

13

c.   *The mechanics of tax collection*

• *tax assessment*

Most tax authorities generally base their assessments of tax liability on the tax returns and the accompanying financial statements the taxpayer submits. The relevant tax authorities may request additional information, further documentary evidence, or both, from the individual or entity. The authorities may also require an audit, in which an official auditor reviews the taxpayer's financial records. The company will be informed in writing by the tax authority regarding the *tax assessment*. Commercially justified expenses incurred by the taxpayer may be allowable deductions for income tax purposes unless a specific rule prohibits the deduction or places a limitation on the amount deducted.

• *tax optimization*
• *tax avoidance*
• *tax evasion*
• *tax fraud*

There are very significant differences among the concepts of *tax optimization, tax avoidance, tax evasion*, and *tax fraud*. Tax optimization involves lawfully planning one's affairs to reduce tax liability. In the US and UK, tax avoidance is also a reduction of tax liability by lawful methods, although some other jurisdictions do not share this view. Tax evasion is an illegal action or activity taken to prevent the lawful assessment of taxes – for example by concealing or failing to declare income. Tax fraud occurs if a tax evasion is committed by using false documents in order to deceive tax authorities.

• *double taxation treaty* • *center of vital interests*	Most tax treaties provide for the determination of residency between two countries. One of the factors to determine individual residency in a *double taxation treaty* is to consider where the taxpayer has a permanent home. However, if a property is owned in one country and an apartment rented in another, and both properties are available for use, the question may not be easily resolved. In such cases the deciding question is to determine where the taxpayer's *center of vital interests* is located. This usually means where the main family life is based.

It has been said that the difference between tax avoidance and tax evasion is the thickness of a prison wall.

The double taxation treaty between the two countries did not address whether social insurance payments can be levied in both jurisdictions.

d.   *Tax havens*

• *tax haven* • *tax shelter* • *nominal taxes* • *shell company* • *transparency*	A *tax haven* or *tax shelter* is a jurisdiction within a state or a territory where taxes are levied at a *nominal* or nil rate of tax, and where individuals and entities can either move physically or establish a presence by way of a subsidiary or *shell company* in order to avoid paying tax. Tax havens are often characterized by very low or non-existent taxes and a lack of *transparency* and no exchange of information with foreign tax authorities.

- *tax exiles*
- *trust*
- *transfer pricing*
- *offshore financial centers*

Tax havens may attract individuals or companies by, for example:

a) Provision of personal residency for wealthy individuals who leave a higher-tax jurisdiction to live in a state that offers significantly lower rates of income tax and often no capital gains tax or inheritance tax. Such individuals are often called *tax exiles*.

b) Asset holding which usually involves the use of a *trust* or a trust company, thereby changing the ownership of the assets and removing them from a higher-tax jurisdiction.

c) Trading activities which, for example, involve re-invoicing from the tax haven and concentrating the profits there instead of in the main sources of customer revenue. Tax authorities seek to counter such activity by more effective *transfer pricing* rules.

d) The deposit of funds with an *offshore financial center* in a tax haven which often then lends the money or re-invests it back into a high tax jurisdiction, charging royalties or administrative fees and retaining profits in the jurisdiction with lower or non-existent taxes.

- *anti-avoidance*

Some tax authorities have enacted *anti-avoidance* legislation that seeks to counter the sheltering of income in tax havens through a combination of transfer pricing measures and restrictions on deductibility, and by taxing the remittance of any amounts returned from the tax haven.

| • *offshore financial centers* • *discretionary trust* | Small, low-tax jurisdictions which specialize in providing financial services to foreign corporations are usually known as *offshore financial centers*. |

In an attempt to minimize the impact of UK inheritance tax on his estate, X established a *discretionary trust* for the purpose of holding his assets on behalf of his children.

B.   Sample Definitions

income tax	Tax levied on the earnings of natural persons.
value added tax	General consumption tax in some jurisdictions that aims to generate revenue from private income and assets spent on consumer goods and services.
double taxation treaty	Agreement under international law between two states that primarily regulates the extent to which the income of natural persons or legal entities resident or based in one state may be taxed in the other state.

C.   Collocations Corner

→ to allow double taxation relief

| to grant a person or company relief from multiple tax charges for the same item of income, based on an agreement between two countries under international law | UK legislation allows non-residents double taxation relief. |

→ to assess tax liability

| to calculate and consider how much tax an individual or corporate entity owes | It was necessary to assess the company's tax liability on an annual basis. |

→ to avoid tax

| to implement legal strategies that reduce the amount of tax owed | He bought a property in Switzerland to avoid tax. |

→ to collect tax

| to call for and gather unpaid taxes from individuals or corporate entities on behalf of the government | The government collected $2,000,000 in taxes. |

→ to contest a finding

| to oppose or dispute a decision on tax liability | He could not contest the Tax Office's finding that he had evaded taxes. |

→ to evade tax

| to intentionally and unlawfully pay less tax than required | The IRS accused the company of evading tax in 2015. |

→ to impose a tax

| to require individuals and corporate entities to contribute to state revenue | The government has raised two billion dollars by imposing taxes on consumer spending. |

→ to incur a penalty

to be subject to punishment as a result of one's own wrongdoing	He incurred a penalty of $4,000 for failing to submit his tax return to the IRS.

→ to levy a tax

to impose a tax	The government levied taxes to raise revenue.

→ to withhold tax

to deduct a portion of income directly before distributing amounts, e.g. dividends or interest to the recipient	The bank withheld tax from its employees' wages.

Personal Notes _____

_____

_____

_____

_____

_____

_____

_____

_____

_____

14 Criminal Law

A. Key Legal Terms

a. *Criminal liability*

• *criminal law* • *criminal liability*	In many civil and common law jurisdictions, codes, federal statutes, or state statutes provide the main basis for prosecuting *criminal law* offenses. Some offenses can give rise to both civil and *criminal liability.*
• *nullum crimen nulla poena sine lege* • *nulla poena sine culpa*	In many countries, criminal liability is based on the principles of *nullum crimen nulla poena sine lege* (no crime or punishment without a law) and *nulla poena sine culpa* (no penalty without guilt).

Some acts may only give rise to criminal liability if the victim of the crime files a formal complaint against the defendant.

Personal Notes _____

_____

_____

_____

_____

_____

b.   Criminal procedure

- *crime*
- *offense*
- *warrant for arrest*
- *summons*
- *search warrant*
- *suspect*
- *extradition*
- *warning*
- *custody*

When a person is suspected of having committed a *crime* he or she may be arrested at the scene of the alleged *offense*, or a court may issue a *warrant for* his or her *arrest*, or he or she may receive a *summons* ordering him or her to appear in court. A *search warrant* may also be issued by a court authorizing police officers to enter and search the premises of a *suspect*. If a suspect leaves the jurisdiction following commission of the alleged crime he or she may be *extradited*. Upon arrest, the suspect may be let off with a *warning* or taken into police *custody* (i.e. apprehended or detained) for questioning. A record may be made in the police station setting out the charges against the suspect. Within a certain period of time the suspect must be taken before a court.

- *the accused*
- *pre-trial detention*
- *trial*
- *criminal proceedings*
- *bail*
- *electronic surveillance*
- *misdemeanors*
- *summary proceedings*
- *felonies*
- *indictable offenses*
- *plea-bargaining*
- *trial by jury*

The court will decide whether the accused should be detained *(pre-trial detention)* until the date set for trial (i.e. *criminal proceedings*), or released on bail in exchange for security (usually money). The accused may also be placed under *electronic surveillance.* For lesser crimes, such as *misdemeanors, summary proceedings* may suffice. More serious crimes, such as felonies, referred to as *indictable offenses,* may be resolved by *plea-bargaining* (admission of guilt on a less serious charge, e.g. manslaughter for murder in favor of a lesser penalty), or will be *tried by jury* in a higher court.

14

- *defendant*
- *counts*
- *indictment*
- *counsel for the prosecution*
- *counsel for the defense*
- *evidence*
- *sworn witness testimony*
- *witness*
- *alibi*
- *to corroborate*
- *presumed innocent*
- *to bear the burden*
- *conviction*
- *actus rea*
- *mens rea*
- *strict liability offense*

Details of the *defendant's* alleged offense(s) are set out, usually in separate *counts*, in the *indictment*. At the trial, *counsel for the prosecution* and *counsel for the defense* present their respective cases and submit their *evidence* in the form of *sworn witness testimony* and exhibits, and may examine and cross-examine their respective *witnesses* one or more of whom may provide an *alibi*, i.e. provide *corroborating* evidence that the accused was elsewhere at the time of the crime. An accused person is generally *presumed innocent*. Consequently, the prosecution *bears the burden* of proving that the defendant is guilty. To secure a *conviction* the prosecution must prove the *actus rea* (the guilty act) as well as *mens rea* (intent or the guilty mind).

This burden-shifting framework does not apply, however, to *strict liability offenses*, in which certain acts impose automatic liability even absent proof of a defendant's intent. Strict liability offenses do not exist in many jurisdictions that recognize the principle of *nulla poena sine culpa*.

- *diminished capacity*
- *verdict*
- *acquitted*
- *released*
- *sentenced*
- *time-barred*
- *Statute of Limitations*
- *criminal liability*

A lesser crime may be attributed to a defendant who successfully raises the defense of *diminished capacity*. If the *verdict* is "not guilty," the defendant is *acquitted* and *released*; if guilty, *sentenced*. Prosecution of a crime committed many years earlier may be *time-barred* under the *Statute of Limitations*. More serious crimes, such as murder, are not generally time-barred.

A company may also be subject to *criminal liability*.

In the US the Statute of Limitations does not apply to *felonies*; hence the *warrant* for Mr Polanski's *arrest* issued by the Los Angeles police force in July 1977 is still pending.

c.   *The perpetrator*

- *perpetrator*
- *suspect*
- *detainee*
- *the accused*
- *defendant*
- *offender*
- *criminal*
- *convict*
- *felon*
- *prisoner*
- *out on probation*
- *fugitive*

The terms relating to the alleged *perpetrator* of a criminal act are many and varied. Some are synonyms, others reflect the stage of criminal proceedings. Hence a person apprehended on suspicion of having committed a crime is the *suspect*; if detained, *detainee*; following formal charges, *the accused*; in court, the *defendant*. Upon conviction the terms *offender, criminal, convict*, or *felon* may apply. A *prisoner* who is released from jail under certain conditions is said to be *out on probation*. A prisoner who escapes imprisonment is a *fugitive*.

Personal Notes _____

_____

_____

_____

_____

_____

_____

_____

_____

d.   *Sanctions/sentence*

- *fine*
- *suspended sentence*
- *probation*
- *community service order*
- *custodial sentence*
- *incarceration*
- *death penalty*
- *capital punishment*
- *petty offenses*
- *misdemeanors*
- *felonies*
- *insanity defense*
- *detained at her/his Majesty's pleasure*
- *life sentence*
- *to commute*
- *parole*
- *good behavior bond*
- *disqualification of a license*
- *forfeiture of assets*

When a defendant is found guilty as charged, he or she may be ordered to pay a *fine*, receive a *suspended sentence*, ordered to perform *community service*, or receive a *custodial sentence* (which can mean the same as imprisonment, detention, and *incarceration*) for a specified time depending on the circumstances of the crime. In some jurisdictions, the defendant may face the *death penalty* (also referred to as *capital punishment*). The penal system in many countries distinguishes among three categories of offenses, which differ in severity and in the criminal penalty they carry (e.g. fines, prison time on probation, or prison time). *Minor* or *petty offenses* are typically punishable by a fine. *Misdemeanors* can carry a relatively short custodial sentence or a monetary penalty. *Felonies* carry a longer custodial sentence, often with a lower chance of early release on parole. In the UK, if an accused successfully raises the *insanity defense*, he or she may be *detained at her/his Majesty's pleasure*, i.e. for an indefinite period of time. A *life sentence* (which, depending on the jurisdiction, may or may not be for life) may be *commuted* to a lesser period. The supervised release of a prisoner before the completion of the sentence is known as *parole*. Other sanctions may include imposing a *good behavior bond, disqualification of a license,* or *forfeiture of assets*.

He received a $5,000 *fine* and was placed on *probation* for two years.

e. Remedies

• *appeal* • *review (or parole) board* • *pardon*	A defendant convicted of a crime may *appeal* against both the verdict and the sentence. A *review board* has the authority to grant, defer, or refuse a prisoner's request for release or parole; the executive authorities may *pardon* a convicted person and order his or her release.

In many countries, the government may pardon a person who has been convicted of a crime when the person has paid his debt to society or is otherwise considered to be deserving of a pardon.

B. Sample Definitions

plea bargain	Agreement between the prosecutor and the defendant in common law criminal proceedings in which the defendant agrees to plead guilty in return for some form of concession from the prosecutor, such as the acceptance of a plea to a lesser charge or a reduced sentence.
criminal liability	A person becomes liable for criminal penalties if his or her conduct (whether an act or omission) conforms with the elements of an offense, is unlawful, and displays the required criminal intent.
search warrant	Written order issued by a prosecutor's office or court permitting a search or examination of the person, premises, objects, or recordings named in the order to be carried out by the investigating authorities, normally the police.

167

C. Collocations Corner

14

→ to accuse someone of a crime

to charge a person with an offense or crime (note – the person may not be guilty)	The prosecution accused Mr. Smith of murder.

→ to acquit of a crime

to find someone not guilty of an offense or crime (by a judge or jury in court)	The jury acquitted the defendant on all charges.

→ to arrest a person

to take a person into custody on reasonable suspicion that this person committed a crime or offense	They arrested him on suspicion of dealing drugs.

→ to be on trial for a crime

to be the subject of legal action in court for a crime or offense	Ms. Jones is on trial for theft.

→ to carry out inquiries

to conduct the examination and investigation of a crime	The Royal Commission will carry out further inquiries into Drug Trafficking (UK).

→ to charge with an offense

to formally accuse of an offense or crime	The prosecution charged Mr. Miller with embezzlement.

→ to commit a criminal offense

to carry out an act that is criminally punishable by law	In vandalizing her neighbor's garage, Ms. Smith committed a criminal offense against her neighbor.

→ to convict of a crime

| to determine that an accused is guilty of an offense or crime (by a judge or jury in court) | The jury convicted the defendant of robbery. |

→ to enter a plea of guilty/not guilty or to plead guilty/not guilty

| to formally admit or deny liability for a criminal offense | The defendant entered a guilty plea on the charges of robbery and manslaughter. |

→ to face prosecution

| to be charged with a criminal offense and face the resulting legal proceedings | Mr. King will face prosecution by the state's most renowned prosecutor. |

→ to face trial

| to be involved in full legal proceedings in court | Mr. King will face trial for manslaughter. |

→ to give evidence on oath

| to swear under oath to provide truthful information and answers that help prove the defendant's innocence or guilt | The witness gave evidence on oath at trial. |

→ to grant bail

| to release an accused from custody until the next court appearance following payment of a sum of money as security | He was granted bail in the sum of $5 million dollars. |

→ to hold in custody

| to keep in police or court detention until a later date, e.g. until a trial or sentencing | The police held him in custody while they waited for his lawyer to arrive. |

14

→ to indict for an offense

| to accuse formally of an offense or crime (by a grand jury) | The grand jury indicted her for fraud. |

→ to overturn a conviction

| to set aside or change a prior guilty verdict | The Court of Appeals overturned his drunk driving conviction. |

→ to put on probation

| to sentence to a period of supervision while remaining in the community, instead of serving prison time | The judge put the defendant on probation for three years. |

→ to rebut a presumption

| to disprove a belief that something is true | The prosecution must rebut the presumption that the defendant is innocent. |

→ to refuse bail

| to formally deny a release from custody until the next court appearance | She was refused bail in light of the high risk she poses to the public. |

→ to release on bail

| to let out of police or court custody, usually following payment of a sum of money as a guarantee that the accused will appear in court | The judge released both suspects on bail on Friday. |

→ to release on parole

| to release a prisoner from jail early based on good behavior, subject to certain conditions and police supervision | He committed murder after he was released on parole. |

14

→ to remand into custody

| to send to police or court detention until a later date, e.g. until a trial or sentencing | The police arrested the suspect and remanded him into custody pending further investigation. |

→ to set a date for trial

| to decide on and declare a date for the commencement of legal proceedings | The judge set a date for trial at the beginning of November. |

→ to submit evidence

| to present formal information or statements that help determine the accused's innocence or guilt | The witness submitted photographs as evidence. |

→ to take into custody

| to apprehend so as to effect legal restraint | The police took the suspect into custody for questioning by investigators. |

Personal Notes _____

_____

_____

_____

_____

_____

_____

_____

Legal Practice
Manuals for Legal Writing

1   Professional Legal Writing – Language and Style

This chapter deals with language for legal memoranda and professional correspondence. Use it to edit and assess these documents critically after your initial draft(s) and to ensure that you are communicating effectively with your audience. Improving your professional language and writing style can also lead to new career possibilities or opportunities for studying abroad. The following sections offer some key ways to review your approach to memoranda and professional correspondence.

A.   Plain Legal English

Professional legal writing in memoranda and correspondence includes substituting Plain Legal English for overly formal and unnecessarily technical language. Plain Legal English refers to an extension of the Plain Language movement, which suggests using simpler and more understandable language in legal documents so that lawyers and non-lawyers can understand these documents more readily.

As lawyers often rely on existing precedents, legal documents can contain "legalese" or "legal jargon" that is incomprehensible to readers not trained in the law. Faced with such technical language, lawyers can simplify important documents by changing their structure and replacing legalese terms with Plain Legal English. Doing so, however, requires great care to ensure that the document retains its intended legal effect. In addition, be aware that digital and social media influence spoken and written language, including language in professional contexts. Practical written communication now tends to be short, and frequently follows straightforward patterns. This style applies especially to email communication, which is often read on a mobile device.

The following sections describe hallmarks of professional legal writing under the Plain Legal English approach.

a.   Clear and concise writing

Above all, professional legal writing must be clear. Writing concisely is the first step toward writing clearly.

First, use each sentence to make only one point. Avoid run-on sentences that address more than one issue.

Second, avoid trying to express the same point in two or more redundant sentences. If two (or more) sentences express a similar meaning, combine them into a single, concise sentence containing all the information necessary to make your point.

Third, keep your sentences short by cutting unnecessary words or phrases. Each sentence should contain no more than 20 to 25 words. Unnecessary words often include lengthy introductory phrases, redundant terminology, long phrases, and abstractions. Try to exclude such language when drafting or revising legal memoranda or professional correspondence. Instead, adopt ordinary and personalized wording, as in the examples below.

EXAMPLES:

Legalese Alternative:
(…) We would be obliged now if you could review said matter described herein having regard to the enclosed and return to us with your further instructions thereon. Also, it should be mentioned that, in the event of the hearing date proceeding before the court then further costs and expenses will arise thereafter, as a witness familiar with the contracts will be required to attend the court. It may be necessary to consider trying to reach a settlement of all the disputes outstanding between the parties. (85 Words)

Plain Legal English Alternative:
(…) Please review this matter in light of the attachments and send us your further instructions. If the court hearing proceeds, further costs will arise. A witness familiar with the contracts will have to attend. We should consider trying to settle the disputes between the parties. (45 words)

In the example above, the Plain Legal English alternative omits excess words and needless introductory phrases. Ordinary wording and Plain English formulations take precedence over complicated phrases and fancy-sounding words. Simpler alternatives and more personal writing replace word pairs and vague, generic statements.

175

Specifically:
- We would be obliged [...] if *becomes* please
- in the event of *becomes* if
- thereon *is omitted, as it adds no additional meaning*
- It should be mentioned that *is omitted, as it adds no additional meaning*
- Costs and expenses *become* costs
- It may be necessary to consider *becomes shorter and more personal as* We should consider

Omit the expressions below in favor of the Plain English terms in parentheses.

Word pairs:
- Last will and testament *(will)*
- Null and void *(void)*
- Each and every *(choose one of the two terms; note that "each" is correct only when there are two items, while "every" is appropriate for two or more items)*

Long phrases:
- Subsequent to *(after)*
- In advance of *(before)*
- A large number of *(many)*
- In the event of *(if)*
- At the current time *(currently)*

Abstractions:
- Contacted *(telephoned, e-mailed, faxed)*
- Law enforcement *(Police)*

Other:
- In order to *(to)*
- It is important to note/state/mention that *(omit this unnecessary prefacing phrase and simply state your point)*

b.   *Tailor your writing style to your audience*

Professional legal writing requires assessing your writing style based on your audience. First, to ensure that your memorandum or professional correspondence accurately describes your intended meaning, consider both the person who will read the document (e.g. a lawyer, judge, lay person, or non-lawyer expert within a specific field) and the document's purpose. Your style will and should differ depending on whether your audience is trained in the law (with a civil law or common law background), works in a specific industry (e.g. the banking sector), or lacks special legal, technical, or professional training.

Second, the culture and language of where you and your audience are based heavily influence your writing style in English. Legal concepts differ among jurisdictions, and also differ with regard to whether they are based in common law or civil law, are mixed common-civil law (e.g. Canada or Hong Kong), or arise from an entirely different legal system (e.g. China). In each system the language and concepts will vary. Give careful consideration to cultural differences among legal systems when you explain legal concepts from your own jurisdiction. Both native and non-native speakers may use words incorrectly or outside of their common usage, particularly if they fail to pay adequate attention to a word's literal meaning. To avoid misunderstandings, think about your reader's perception of the document and use simple yet precise words that he or she will easily understand.

Translating words' and concepts' meaning between and among jurisdictions.

Lawyers who are not native English speakers often borrow Legal English terms to explain concepts in their own jurisdictions. While this approach may suffice, be aware that borrowing Legal English terminology to explain foreign legal concepts carries certain risks. The reader may incorrectly infer a particular meaning from your choice of words, and will thereby interpret a term or phrase to mean something different from the meaning you intended to give that term or phrase. To avoid this risk, consider choosing terms or phrases which explain, describe, or define the concept in a more functional manner.

For example, the term "Mortgage," a traditional form of security in real estate in the common law, may roughly correspond to similar types of security in some civil law systems (e.g. the "Hypothek" in German property law). Depending on your audience, using the term "Mortgage" may be sufficient, as it indicates clearly that you mean a form of security against land. However, a closer look at the respective concepts and their evolution shows that they are quite different. The "Hypothek" originated in Roman law, while the "Mortgage" developed in the courts of law and equity in England and other common law countries. Depending on the context, it may be necessary to point out or explain the differences and similarities between the legal concepts and their ramifications for a particular transaction.

Subtle differences to words can impact what your writing means:
Be aware of commonly confused terms such as *ensure, assure,* and *insure; counsel* and *council; principal* and *principle;* and *guarantee* and *guaranty.*

177

1

c. *Make your sentences readable and convincing*

Choose verbs over nouns

Whenever possible, choose a verb, adjective, or adverb over a noun or noun phrase. Replace nouns ending in "ion" with a verb unless you are referring to a procedure, e.g. "the litigation procedure."

Example	The creditor must make an application to the court for substituted service of the proceedings on the debtor.
Change to	The creditor must *apply* to the court for substituted service of the proceedings on the debtor.

Subject-Verb-Object order

Whenever possible, group the subject, verb, and object together at the start of the sentence. Where a long sentence contains numerous qualifications or conditions, consider listing such qualifications or conditions in a separate sentence.

Example	*Sentence with Qualifications/Conditions:* If a company becomes insolvent, the directors, at the request of the court or the examiner, at any time after receipt of notice, must disclose its latest financial dealings and accounts.
Consider instead	The directors [subject] must disclose [verb] the latest financial dealings and accounts [object] of an insolvent company. This obligation arises at the request of the court or the examiner and at any time after receipt of notice.

The verb "to be"
Limit the use of weak expressions using "to be" and its conjugated forms to create a more concise sentence structure and more lively writing.

Example	The parties *are in agreement* that the corporation's liability *is dependent* on whether its actions *were violative of* the law.
Consider instead	The parties *agree* that the corporation's liability *depends on* whether its actions *violated* the law.

Prepositions
Reduce prepositions within sentences.

Example	This court did not err in issuing its order *of* dismissal *of* the claims *of* the plaintiff.
Consider instead	This court did not err in dismissing the plaintiff's claims.

Active v. passive voice
In general, choose the active over the passive voice. However, the passive voice may be acceptable in some instances, i.e. if you intentionally want to make your writing less direct, to conceal the parties responsible for an action or a decision, or to deliberately focus on an object rather than a subject.

Example	An objection *was entered* by the plaintiff's lawyers regarding the manner of questioning, but the objection *was overruled* by the judge.
Consider instead	The plaintiff's lawyers *objected* to the manner of questioning, but the judge *overruled* the objection.

1

Sentence emphasis – the "power position"

Place the point you wish to emphasize at the end of your sentence. Correspondingly, to weaken or downplay an issue, place it in a dependent clause at the beginning of a sentence.

Example 1	*To emphasize that the plaintiff's injury occurred in a particular jurisdiction:* The plaintiff incurred severe injuries last July while he was in Switzerland. *To emphasize the plaintiff's injury:* Last July, while he was in Switzerland, the plaintiff incurred severe injuries. *To emphasize when the plaintiff's injury occurred:* The plaintiff incurred severe injuries while he was in Switzerland last July.
Example 2	His actions were not against the law, but they raised ethical questions. *(Placing the ethically questionable nature of the actions in the "power position" at the end of the sentence emphasizes the actions' negative ethical ramifications.)* *To downplay the actions' ethically questionable nature and emphasize instead that the actions were legal, rearrange the sentence to read:* His actions raised ethical questions, but they were not against the law. *or* While his actions raised ethical questions, they were not against the law.

Negatives and double negatives

Your writing will become more concise and livelier if you can change negative-form verbs into positive-form verbs (Example 1). In addition, avoid double negatives wherever possible to avoid overly complex structures and redundant terminology (Example 2).

Example 1	*Negative Form:* He did not have the necessary qualifications for the position. *Positive form:* He lacked the necessary qualifications for the position.
Example 2	*Negative Form:* The issues between the parties to the dispute were not uncontroversial. *Positive form:* The issues between the parties to the dispute were controversial.

Describing parties:

It is common practice in professional legal writing to use the parties' real names rather than their legal descriptions. To avoid confusion and to personalize your language, avoid overusing terminology such as "plaintiff and defendant" or "mortgagor and mortgagee" in favor of using the parties' names where possible. In addition, be careful to avoid potentially ambiguous formulations when using pronouns (see Part II, Chapter 8, Contract Drafting, pp. 216–239).

Example	The court asked *the mortgagor* to provide *the mortgagor's* affidavit to *the mortgagee* within 21 days of the court's judgment.
Consider instead	The court asked *Mr. Smith* to provide *his* affidavit to Ms. Jones within 21 days of the judgment.

2 Formal v. Informal Correspondence

Phrases and Expressions

These phrases and expressions are appropriate for both emails and letters. Depending on the context and on the recipient of your message, you can use either formal or informal language in an email. However, a letter calls for formal language in most circumstances.

A. Introduction

Informal	Formal
• Hi/Hello/Hi [*name*]	• Dear [*name*]
	• Dear Sir(s)/Madam
	• Dear Mr [*name*]/Ms [*name*] (US: Dear Mr. [*name*]/Dear Ms. [*name*])
	Note: In the US, the term "Ms." is commonly used to address women with whom you are not on a first-name basis. The terms "Mrs." and "Miss" are considered outdated in written correspondence. Further, the term "Miss" may even be deemed condescending and may cause offense.

B.   Referring To A Previous Communication

Informal	Formal
• I wanted to tell you/write to you …	• I am writing to follow up on our telephone conversation/ your request/our discussion on [*date*] regarding …
• As I said/mentioned on the telephone earlier, …	• I am writing in/with reference to your email/letter/telephone call of [*date*], in which you requested advice on …
• As we talked about, …	• Further to our telephone conversation of 12 June 2016 (US: June 12, 2016)/this morning/last week/yesterday …
• You asked …	• I write in response to your question/your query/ your inquiry regarding the professional services our law firm can provide.
• Thanks for asking about our law firm's services.	• We recently received your letter dated [*date*] regarding …
• We got your letter/email about …	• Thank you for your email/ letter of [*date*].

C.   Transmitting Documents

Informal	Formal
• Here is [*document name*].	• Attached please find [*document name*].
• I'm sending you [*document name*].	• Enclosed please find [*document name*].
• I've added [*document name*] as an attachment.	• For the purpose of (US: for purposes of) your review, I have attached [*document name*] to this message.
• I'm attaching [*document*] to this email.	• For your reference/review, I am enclosing a copy of [*document name*].

D.   Requests To The Recipient

Informal	Formal
• Can you/will you …?	• Could you please/would you please …?
• Tell me/let me know …	• Could you please let us know/ would you mind telling me …?
• What information do you need from us?	• Could you inform us of any additional information you may need from us?
• Please send us …	• We would appreciate it if you could please send us … • It would be very helpful if you could send us …

• I need to know which documents you want/Which documents do you want?	• Could you please advise us/ Kindly advise us which, if any, documents you still require?
• Let me know as soon as you can/right away/a.s.a.p. (as soon as possible)…	• I would be very grateful if/I would appreciate it if you could let us know as soon as possible/by [date]
• Can you look into this issue?	• Could you investigate/research this issue?
Note: While a.s.a.p. is common in informal correspondence and speech, it sets a forceful and impolite tone. Avoid a.s.a.p. in client communications.	*Note: The term "Kindly" is not used very frequently in the United States.*

E.   Closing Phrases

Informal	Formal
• Thanks/Thanks a lot.	• Thank you again for the chance to represent you in this case/for your business/for the opportunity to handle this matter for you.
• That's it for now.	• Please call/telephone me at your convenience should you have any questions whatsoever, or should you wish to discuss the matter in more detail.

• Bye.	• I look forward to hearing from you regarding next steps/ dates on which you might be available for a meeting.
• See you.	• I would be pleased/happy to discuss this matter with you in more detail. • I send you my very best personal regards. (US only)
• Talk to you tomorrow/next week.	• As always, I am at your disposal should you have any questions. (US only)

F.   Miscellaneous Phrases for Use in the Main Portion of the Communication

Informal	Formal
• We have to/need to talk about …	• It is important/imperative/ crucial that we discuss …
• I want/wanted to ask about …	• I would like to inquire (UK: enquire) about …
• I need to know if you will agree to …	• I would like to confirm whether you will agree to …
• We are in a bit of a hurry/ really in a hurry here/on this point. • We have to move fast on this issue.	• Time is of the essence on this point. • It is essential that we move on this issue soon.

• I'd like to talk to you about the services we could offer you.	• I would welcome the opportunity to discuss with you how we might be able to assist you.
• When can you meet with us?	• When would you be/are you available for a meeting?
• Does tomorrow at 1p.m. work for a telephone call?	• Would you be/are you available tomorrow at 1p.m. for a telephone call?
• We can help you with this issue.	• We are able to assist you in resolving this issue.
• I'd like to fill you in on the details. • Can you fill me in on what happened at the meeting?	• I would like to provide you with an update on/an overview of/an explanation of the details. • Could you provide me with an update on/could you provide me with the details of what occurred/transpired at the meeting?
• What do you think about …?	• I would appreciate hearing your thoughts on …
• We have to figure this issue out.	• We have to resolve this issue/ find a resolution/reach a resolution.
• Let's get in touch later this week.	• I suggest we set up a time to meet/a time for a telephone conference later this week.
• I am happy to tell you that …	• It is my pleasure to tell/inform you that …

3   Professional Correspondence

A.   Technical Aspects

a.   *Salutations*

In professional correspondence, address the recipient of your letter or email with the phrase "Dear *[recipient's name]*." Unless you and the recipient have been exchanging a series of short, casual emails, avoid starting a letter or email with the more informal terms "Hi *[name]*," "Hello *[name]*," or the recipient's name only *[Suzanne:]*. Be sure to include a comma or a colon after the salutation, keeping in mind that a colon creates a sterner tone than using a comma:

- *Dear Suzanne,*
- *Dear Suzanne:*
- *Dear Ms. Lowell,*
- *Dear Ms. Lowell:*

b.   *First name or last name*

Use your judgment, based on prior communications and your relationship with the recipient, on whether to address the recipient by his or her first (Dear Suzanne) or last name (Dear Ms. Lowell). Do not use both the first and last names (Dear Suzanne Lowell). Such a formulation would be highly unusual and might raise suspicions that the letter was auto-generated, rather than drafted by a lawyer.

c.   *Appellations*

When addressing male recipients by their last name, use **Mr.** *[last name]* in the US and **Mr** *[last name]* in the UK. For female recipients, regardless of age, position, or marital status, professional business correspondence in the US requires that you use the appellation **Ms.** *[last name]*, rather than the old-fashioned terms Mrs. or Miss. In the UK, both the modern term **Ms** *[last name]* and the appellation **Mrs** *[last name]* are acceptable in professional correspondence. *Note that the terms Mr. and Ms. have a period in the US, while Mr, Ms, and Mrs do not need a period in the UK.*

Choosing the correct appellation can be difficult when you are addressing multiple individuals in a single email or business letter. The format you choose will depend on how well you know the individuals in question, and how formal or casual you wish to sound. Consider choosing from among the following options:

Dear All, or Dear all,	Appropriate for an email in which you know the recipients reasonably well. Note that Dear Both/both is highly unusual and would strike many readers as incorrect.
Dear Suzanne, Dear John,	Appropriate for an email in which you know the recipients reasonably well. Note that using the recipient's names rather than "Dear All" gives your email a warmer, more personal touch.
Dear Ms. Lowell, Dear Mr. Lowell,	Appropriate for an email or a letter in which you intend to convey a more formal tone.

d. Titles

Unless you are addressing a medical doctor, it is uncommon in professional correspondence in the US to include titles such as Dr. or Prof. in the appellation. If you do include a title, note that, unlike in several other countries, your appellation should include only the highest title the recipient holds. Thus, an appellation such as "Prof. Dr. Jones" would be sufficiently unusual to be considered incorrect in professional correspondence from a lawyer. *Note that the titles Dr. and Prof. both have a period in the US, while only the term Prof. has a period in the UK.*

e.   Dates

Note that the format for dates differs between the US and the UK, as follows:

US	UK
• January 15, 2016	• 15 January 2016
• 1/15/2016	• 15/1/2016

f.   Signoffs

Numerous rules, some archaic and some still in use in practice, exist regarding the appropriate signoff for correspondence. In modern professional correspondence, we suggest choosing one of the following options, making sure to place a comma after the sign-off phrase and before your name:

- *Best regards,*
- *Kind regards,*
- *Regards,*
- *Sincerely yours,*
- *Sincerely,*

For a far more personal touch, you may also consider one of the following sign-off phrases:

- *Warm regards,*
- *Best wishes,*

Note that a US recipient of business correspondence may consider a sign-off such as "Yours faithfully" or "Respectfully yours" old-fashioned.

B.   Tips on Structuring & Drafting Correspondence

This section provides an approach to structuring professional correspondence. Use it to plan and outline your professional correspondence, keeping in mind your specific audience.

Practical legal writing always benefits from a clear structure, as well-structured correspondence is easier for the reader to follow and more convincing. Imposing a defined structure on your writing also forces you, as the drafter, to identify, organize, and then arrange your thoughts and logical reasoning completely and clearly.

Outlining the structure you will use in advance will help you save time and effort, both of which you will need for one or more rounds of edits. Planning what structure to use before you start writing also helps to prevent errors in logic or reasoning, omitting logical steps or conclusions, lumping separate issues together, or redundantly addressing a single issue multiple times. A solid structure, thus, serves as a checklist to confirm that your thought process, reasoning, and conclusions are sound.

a.   *Introduction*

Your introductory sentence should state why you are writing, which most often involves a reference to prior correspondence or other communication with the recipient of your letter. Referring to prior correspondence or an earlier conversation will help the reader recall the issues you previously discussed, and will allow him or her to locate and reread relevant prior correspondence if doing so will help to provide context for the current letter. Consider one of the following approaches to drafting an introductory sentence:

I am writing
- to follow up on […]
- in/with reference to […]
- in/with regard to […]
- in response to […]

OR

Thank you for your letter dated […]/inquiry regarding […]. We are pleased to assist you in this matter/with regard to this question.
(See Part II, Chapter 2, Formal v. Informal Correspondence, Section B, p. 183, for more examples.)

b.   *Transmitting Documents*

Use one of the following formulations when you send additional documents along with your correspondence.

Letters	Emails
• Please find enclosed […] for your review/for your reference/for your files.	• Please find attached […] for your review/for your reference/for your files.
• Enclosed please find […] for your review/for your reference/for your files.	• Attached please find […] for your review/for your reference/for your files.
• I am enclosing […] for your review/for your reference/for your files.	• I am attaching […] for your review/for your reference/for your files.

(See Part II, Chapter 2, Formal v. Informal Correspondence, Section C, p. 184, for more examples.)

c. *Presenting the Issues*

Before you start writing, draw up a list of every issue and sub-issue you will address to avoid missing crucial points and to help you clarify how different issues relate to one another.

Next, determine the order in which you will address the issues. While it is common to lead with the most important issue, keep in mind that what the writer considers most important may not be the same issue which matters most to the recipient. If the recipient of your correspondence is likely to be anxious about a particular issue (significant payments, legal liability, inability to pursue a desired course of action), address this point upfront, even if there are other issues you consider more important. In addition, resolving the primary issue or issues at play may depend on resolving a series of other, less significant issues. In such cases, consider starting with a one-line or two-line "short answer" on the primary issue, noting that the primary issue hinges on a number of sub-issues. Identify and discuss each sub-issue, including how each sub-issue relates to resolving the primary issue, and then set out your overall conclusions.

Once you have identified all the issues you plan to address, as well as the order in which you intend to cover them, draft a brief introductory roadmap at the beginning of the document. This roadmap should identify the legal issues your correspondence addresses and can also – very briefly – set out your primary conclusion. In this way, the roadmap serves as a frame through which the recipient will read your correspondence and steers the reader's attention to the most important issues.

> **Examples of a short opening paragraph setting out the issues.**
> - In your email dated [Date], you asked us to advise you on the possibilities of filing a successful breach of contract claim based on the facts provided, and more specifically based on the conduct of your suppliers. After researching the issue, and based on the facts and documents you provided, we believe that a claim could be successful and that a court would conclude that the supplier's conduct was a breach of contract. I will explain this conclusion further below after setting out the facts as I currently understand them. (…)
> - Thank you for your letter of [Date] addressed to [addressee] in which you requested advice on recent employment law and particularly how recent changes to the law in this area are likely to impact on your business. Below, we have made some general observations before setting out your specific questions followed by our answers. (…)
> - It was a pleasure to meet with you and your partner yesterday. I hope that we were able to answer your initial questions. As discussed, I am attaching a first draft of the partnership agreement based on your instructions. Please note my observations below. In addition, as I will explain below, I believe that it would also be prudent for your business to take out public liability insurance. (…)

d.   *Background Facts*

Professional legal correspondence often includes a brief recitation of facts to provide context. As clients are looking to you for legal advice and solutions, keep this section short and include only those facts that are relevant to your analysis. Present background information in chronological order and link related issues.

Including facts in professional correspondence serves a twofold purpose. First, this section allows you to clarify that you are basing your analysis and recommendation(s) on a particular set of facts. In so doing, you make it clear that your analysis may change if (1) you did not receive all the relevant facts or (2) new events occur, changing the salient facts on which your analysis relies, and consequently changing your analysis. Second, including background facts in your draft helps you, as a writer, to confirm you are not missing any facts, are not incorrectly assuming any facts to be true that you should not assume to be true, and are taking all relevant facts into consideration in your legal assessment.

Phrases such as "as you described the facts to us," "you explained that," "as we discussed," or "as you mentioned in our conversation last Thursday/your letter dated October 12, 2016" (highlighted in the examples below) are useful, as they indicate how and from whom you obtained the facts (e.g. from the client – often the recipient of the correspondence).

> **Example of background facts in professional correspondence:**
>
> - (...)
>
>   *As you described the facts to us,* Ms. Silber began her employment as the IT manager for Stone's Zurich location on May 1, 2013. Consistent with Swiss law, Ms. Silber's employment contract provided that she was subject to a one month probationary period, during which Stone had the right to terminate Ms. Silber's employment for performance reasons upon seven days' notice. *You explained that* Stone terminated Ms. Silber's employment four weeks after her start date because she did not in fact possess the expertise necessary for the IT manager position, and because you learned that she had misstated her qualifications during the interview process.
>
> - (...)
>
>   *As we discussed,* the action arose out of an incident at work in the early hours of Monday, September 27, 2016 in which you were injured after falling from a ladder at [address] while in the course of your employment with XYZ Limited. You advised us that since the accident you have been receiving treatment from various doctors and that you have been attending physical therapy.

e.   Presenting Your Analysis

The analysis section should be as brief as possible, straightforward, and practically oriented. A client will only want to know that you have done your research, what her options are, and what advantages and disadvantages each option offers. The analysis should lead the reader to your conclusion and recommendation.

Introduction

After briefly presenting the relevant background facts, introduce your legal analysis of the issues at hand. Consider using phrases such as "under the facts as you explained them to us," "based on the above-mentioned facts," or "per your instructions," as they limit your advice based on the information you currently have.

Addressing Individual Legal Issues

When dealing with longer professional correspondence involving numerous legal issues, use headings, sub-headings, and numbering. Using these tools makes your reasoning more accessible to the reader, allowing him or her to read (or skim) your writing in clearly distinguishable sections.

Start each paragraph or section with a topic sentence containing the paragraph's main topic or idea. Move any statements that do not relate to the paragraph's main topic or idea to a separate paragraph with a different topic sentence.

Keep your analysis of each issue separate, except to the extent that a legal issue you have already addressed affects your analysis of a subsequent legal issue. Unless you can address a particular issue in a single sentence, consider presenting your analysis of each issue in a separate paragraph. For each legal issue, (1) state the applicable legal rule, (2) provide a brief explanation of the legal rule, if necessary, and (3) apply the legal rule to the facts at hand to present and discuss your proposed course of action.

Linking Legal Issues

Link your sentences and paragraphs so your reader easily can follow your train of thought and recognize new issues. Common linking words for use within a paragraph include "moreover," "furthermore," "further," and "in addition."

While you can certainly also use "moreover," "furthermore," "further," or "in addition" to link separate paragraphs dealing with distinct legal issues, we recommend simply numbering the issues you are analyzing instead, i.e.

"First," "Second," "Third." A numbering approach improves readability by clarifying whether issues are entirely separate, or whether you are addressing multiple considerations that refer to a single legal issue. If you number the legal issues in your analysis section, make sure you use the numbering approach consistently. Avoid the temptation to use "Finally" for the last issue if you have been using "First," "Second," "Third" up until that point.

When presenting and assessing your proposed course of action, address any difficulties or concerns your approach may raise. Acknowledge any such concerns, and explain why your approach is superior to the alternatives. If necessary, make connections to analogous issues to help the recipient understand your analysis.

Example of analysis

- (…)

   Under the facts as you explained them to us, a court would likely apply well-settled Swiss law that an employer may terminate an employee for performance-based reasons during the probationary period as long as the employer provides the required seven-day notice. In addition, a court will likely take into consideration that, under the law, obtaining a position under false pretenses constitutes a valid basis for termination.

- (…)

   Based on the above-mentioned facts, it is now possible to commence court proceedings against the debtor company. This will increase the pressure on them to deal with your claim, and may lead to a proposal for settlement. In addition, on obtaining a favorable judgement in court, it is possible to make an application for a judicial lien over the debtor's company premises.

---

f.   *Conclusion & Recommendation*

Clients will need to know their options, what each option offers them (as outlined in your analysis section(s)), and your recommendation. While your analysis of each legal issue should include your recommendation on a proposed course of action, correspondence that involves numerous legal issues, particularly when those issues affect one another, should include a brief summary of your overall conclusions. As is true of a research memorandum, your conclusion should not include any new facts, issues, or arguments.

Stay mindful that the decision which alternative to choose is always the client's. The language you choose to phrase your recommendation should reflect this fact. You may also want to ask the recipient of your letter for comments, or for his or her response to the options you propose. In doing so, choose expressions that reflect both your respect for the client and your confidence in your work.

Examples – Conclusion and Recommendation
- In conclusion, I believe, based on my research, that we can argue (…)
- It is, thus, likely/unlikely/probable/very probable that (…)
- We recommend/suggest/think it would be more/most advantageous, think you would benefit from; think […] would be beneficial (…) *(More neutral)*
- We strongly recommend/suggest (doing/choosing/pursuing…) is (not "would be") the most productive course of action/is by far the better option (…) *(More forceful)*

Examples – Asking for comments
- I look forward to your response/your comments.
- I look forward to hearing your thoughts on [this proposal/the proposed course of action].
- I would appreciate hearing your thoughts on […].
- I welcome any comments you may have.

NOT: *Please do not hesitate to contact us regarding any questions or concerns you might have.* This stock formulation shows that you put little effort into writing the last portion of your letter, and may lead the client to wonder whether he or she should, in fact, have concerns about your work. Do yourself a favor and do not raise that question.

NOT: *I look forward to your feedback.* The term "feedback" implies that the person providing feedback is judging – not simply assessing – the work in question. Terms such as "comments" or "response" are more neutral, and, thus, preferable.

---

g.   *Closing Phrases*

Your final line should refer to any additional follow-up, such as a telephone call or meeting in the near future. If possible, suggest specific dates and times on which you will be available for a telephone call or meeting. (See Part II, Chapter 2, Formal v. Informal Correspondence, Section E, pp. 185–186, for a list of useful closing phrases.)

4   Substantive Correspondence to a Client

This template for correspondence to a client (1) summarizing a matter, (2) assessing your client's position, and (3) suggesting a further course of action can be used in a letter or in an email.

It is common practice to send the letter by mail or delivery service, and also to attach a copy of the letter in .pdf format to an email message, for immediate delivery, with the subject header "Correspondence regarding …" and a short note such as the following: "Please find attached correspondence regarding … A hard copy of this correspondence shall follow by first-class mail/UPS/FedEx."

A.   Model Letter for the US

July 20, 2016

VIA EMAIL and FIRST-CLASS MAIL
Ms. Sarah Stone
Stone Technology, LLC
100 Madison Avenue, Suite 700
New York, NY 10007

Re: Wrongful Termination Complaint of
Siena Silber against Stone Technology, LLC

Dear Sarah:

Thank you for retaining us to handle the defense of the wrongful termination lawsuit against Stone Technology, LLC ("Stone") by the former IT manager for Stone's New York office, Ms. Siena Silber. You have asked for our assessment of Ms. Silber's claim that her termination violates New York state employment law. After reviewing Ms. Silber's Complaint with reference to New York state law, and based on the facts you provided, I believe you have strong arguments that Stone's termination of Ms. Silber's employment was entirely lawful. I will explain this conclusion below. As you described the facts to us, Ms. Silber began her employment as the IT manager for Stone's New York location on May 1, 2016. Consistent with New York state law, Ms. Silber's employment contract provided that she was subject to a one-month probationary period, during which Stone had the right to terminate Ms. Silber's employment for performance reasons upon seven days' notice. You explained that Stone terminated Ms. Silber's employment four weeks after her start date because Ms. Silber did not in fact possess the expertise necessary for the IT manager position, and because you learned that she had misstated her qualifications during the interview process.

Under the facts as you explained them to us, a court would be likely to apply the well-settled law that an employer may terminate an employee for performance-based reasons during the probationary period as long as the employer provides the required seven-day notice. In addition, a court will be likely to take into consideration that, under the law, obtaining a position under false pretenses constitutes a valid basis for termination.

Here, applying these legal rules supports the conclusion that Stone acted appropriately. First, Stone terminated Ms. Silber's employment for performance reasons, at a time when the one-month probationary period set forth in Ms. Silber's employment contract was still in effect. Second, Stone provided the requisite seven-day notice period. Third, Stone also discharged Ms. Silber because of her dishonesty during the interview process. For all of these reasons, a court would be likely to rule that Stone did not violate New York state law when it terminated Ms. Silber's employment.

As a result, it is my assessment that Ms. Silber's claim against Stone has little, if any, merit, and that Stone has a good chance of prevailing. Accordingly, I suggest filing an Answer to the Complaint, rather than engaging in settlement negotiations with Ms. Silber. Alternatively, you could offer Ms. Silber a nuisance value settlement lower than the cost of preparing and filing the Answer.

As the response to the Complaint is due by August 15, 2016, I would appreciate hearing from you in the next week, to allow for sufficient time to prepare the response. I am available to discuss the matter on any day next week, and you can reach me by email or by telephone. I look forward to your reply, and will keep you informed of any developments in this matter.

Best regards,

Karina Hirscher

B. Model Letter for the UK

20 July 2016

By EMAIL and FIRST-CLASS MAIL
Ms Sarah Stone
Stone Technology, LLC
100 Madison Avenue, Suite 700
New York, NY 10007

Dear Ms Stone

Wrongful Termination Complaint
Siena Silber v Stone Technology LLC

Thank you for instructing us in the matter of the wrongful termination lawsuit against Stone Technology LLC ("Stone") by the former IT manager for Stone's New York office, Ms Siena Silber.

(…)

Yours sincerely

Karina Hirscher

C. Other Model Sentences

a. *Assessing your client's position: alternative formulations*

aa) Favorable assessment

- In light of the previous court decisions on this issue, it is my opinion that …
- The law/previous court decisions/evidence support(s) your position that …
- You have solid grounds for claiming that …
- You can make out a good argument for your position that …
- There is ample support in the law for your view that …
- You can put forward several strong defenses to this claim …
- I am confident that you have a good chance of prevailing in this matter.

bb)   Unfavorable assessment

- Unfortunately, there is little law/evidence to support …
- My research indicates that it will be difficult to argue that …
- Given the law on this question, we face an uphill battle …
- In light of the law, you are unlikely to prevail on this claim.

b.   *Suggesting a course of action: alternative formulations*

- Accordingly, I propose/suggest …
- Given …, it would be wise to …
- Therefore, you would benefit from …
- I would recommend pursuing an aggressive defense strategy/filing counterclaims/considering a settlement.
- It would be to your advantage to …
- You may want to settle quickly/vigorously fight this claim/adopt a wait-and-see strategy.

c.   *Useful phrases for correspondence to a new client*

- We would be pleased to handle/take on this matter.
- We appreciate the opportunity to assume the defense of this case for you.
- My colleague … and I have significant experience with matters of this nature.
- Should you decide to retain (UK: instruct) our firm, we would recommend the following approach to this case: …
- I would like to discuss our suggested approach with you by telephone/ in person at your convenience.
- We propose staffing this matter/this case with a team consisting of one partner, one senior associate, and one junior associate. Their rates are as follows: [Partner] – $/hour; [Senior Associate] – $/hour; [Junior Associate] – $/hour.
- We anticipate that the associate(s) on the case will perform as much of the work as possible to control costs.
- We are open to an alternative fee arrangement.
- I am enclosing an engagement letter and retainer agreement (UK: client care letter) for your review and execution.

5   Substantive Correspondence to Opposing Counsel

This template for correspondence to your opponent's counsel can be used in a letter or in an email.

To ensure that your opposing counsel receives your correspondence immediately – which may trigger response deadlines on his or her part – it is common practice to send the letter by mail or delivery service, and also to attach a copy of the letter in .pdf format to an email message, for immediate delivery, with the subject header "Correspondence regarding …" and a short note such as the following: "Please find attached correspondence regarding … A hard copy of this correspondence will follow by first-class mail/ UPS/FedEx."

In addition (at least in the US), it is considered acceptable to send the entire correspondence in an email rather than in a letter, particularly if there are numerous and frequent exchanges of correspondence on both sides.

A.   Accepting a Proposal

a.   *Model letter for the US*

July 20, 2016

VIA EMAIL and OVERNIGHT COURIER
John Dewey
Dewey Cheatem & Howe, LLP
1600 California Street, Suite 700
New York, NY 10007

Re: Blackcorner, Inc.'s Acquisition of Greenstone Enterprises, Inc.

Dear John:

I am writing on behalf of my clients, Greenstone Enterprises, Inc. ("Greenstone") and its CEO, Bob Smith, in response to your

July 10, 2016 correspondence in the above-referenced matter. In your letter, you proposed that, following the acquisition of Greenstone, (1) Blackcorner would provide Mr. Smith with a lump-sum payment of USD 750,000 in return for his agreement to resign as CEO; and (2) Blackcorner would retain Greenstone's current sales force in comparable positions. You also provided us with draft provisions, to be included in the merger agreement, addressing these two issues in more detail.

My clients have authorized me to state that they agree to both of your proposals. Following review, we do not have any changes to the language of the provisions you drafted. Accordingly, please incorporate these provisions, as currently drafted, into the merger agreement.

It is my belief that we have now reached agreement on all points at issue in Blackcorner's proposed acquisition of Greenstone. Please advise me by July 30, 2016 whether you believe any outstanding issues remain to be resolved. Otherwise, I look forward to receiving the final version of the merger agreement for execution by my clients.

Best regards,

Sidney Stone

Encl.

Personal Notes _____

_____

_____

_____

_____

_____

_____

b. Model letter for the UK

5

20 July 2016

BY EMAIL and OVERNIGHT COURIER
Mr John Dewey
Dewey Cheatem & Howe LLP
1600 California Street, Suite 700
New York, NY 10007

Dear Mr Dewey

Blackcorner Inc.'s Acquisition of Greenstone Enterprises Inc.

On behalf of my clients, Greenstone Enterprises Inc. ("Greenstone") and its CEO, Bob Smith, I am writing in response to your 10 July 2016 correspondence in the above-mentioned matter.

(…)

Yours sincerely

Sidney Stone

Encl.

The following sections contain alternative formulations for certain portions of the letter, allowing you to tailor your correspondence to the substance you intend to convey.

B. Accepting a Proposal in Part

- While we agree with your proposals in principal, we cannot agree to the language of the provision as it is currently drafted, as/because …
- Thus, we propose the following alternative language.
- While my clients agree to your proposal that …, Mr. Smith will not agree to … As an alternative, we propose that …
- Although we agree that …, we have made some proposed modifications of the language at issue. Please advise us by [*date*] whether your client agrees to these modifications.

C.   Rejecting a Proposal and Offering Alternatives

- Unfortunately, we cannot agree to your proposals.
- My client has instructed me to make the following alternative proposal(s): …
- We suggest the following alternative.
- We cannot agree to certain portions of the draft provisions you prepared. Consequently, I am enclosing documents setting forth alternative language for your review.
- Please advise by [*date*] whether your clients will agree to the alternative provisions enclosed herewith.
- Should your clients disagree with the alternative language we propose, please call me by [*date*] so that we may discuss a possible resolution of these issues.

D.   "Papering the File," i.e. Documenting an Oral Agreement in Writing

- Thank you for your telephone call/making time to meet earlier today.
- I am writing to confirm certain points on which we agreed in our telephone conversation/our meeting this morning.
- First, we agreed that … Second/in addition, we decided that …
- Based on the agreement we reached in our telephone conversation/our meeting on [*date*], I intend to …
- I have prepared the enclosed documents based on our agreement in our telephone conversation/our meeting on [*date*] that …

E.   Requesting Documents or Records

- Before we can agree to the provisions you propose, we require copies of …
- In order to evaluate your proposals properly, we will have to review your client's financial records dating back to 2009.
- Please provide us with copies of the documents at issue by [*date*], so that we may …
- You previously agreed to provide copies of the relevant documents. However, we have not yet received these documents. Accordingly, please send them to us by [*date*].

6 Response to a Request for Documents or Information

This template for a response to a request for information or documents can be used in both civil and criminal cases, in the context of regulatory investigations, and in the context of private litigation. It may also be used in response to requests for the production of witnesses.

A. Agreeing to the Request

a. *Model letter for the US*

July 20, 2016

VIA OVERNIGHT COURIER AND FIRST-CLASS MAIL

Mr. Seymour Stratham
Head of Investigations
Securities & Exchange Commission
100 F Street, N.E.
Washington, D.C. 20549

Re: Investigation of First Municipal Bank File No. 123456

Dear Mr. Stratham:

I represent First Municipal Bank with regard to the investigation referenced above, File No. 123456. I am writing in response to your July 1, 2016 notice, which we received on July 4, 2016, requesting records of all correspondence between and among the officers of First Municipal Bank for the time period of January 1, 2011 to the present.

My client intends to cooperate fully with this investigation, and, therefore, agrees to provide you with copies of the complete set of documents you request. We are currently locating and retrieving all documents responsive to your notice from First Municipal

Bank's physical and electronic archives. Given the significant volume of this set of documents, we anticipate that the process of retrieving the requested correspondence will take at least a month. Thus, we expect that First Municipal Bank will be in a position to provide you with the requested set of documents by August 31, 2016. We will notify you in advance if First Municipal Bank is unable to complete the document collection process by that date.

In the meantime, please do not hesitate to contact me at any time, either by telephone at 212-444-1234 or via email at sstone@Banking-Law.com, should you wish to discuss the status of the document collection or any other aspect of the pending investigation.

Best regards,

Sidney Stone

b.   Model letter for the UK

20 July 2016

BY OVERNIGHT COURIER AND FIRST-CLASS MAIL

Mr Seymour Stratham
Head of Investigations
Securities & Exchange Commission
100 F Street, N.E.
Washington, D.C. 20549

Dear Mr Stratham

Investigation of First Municipal Bank File No. 123456

With regard to the above-mentioned investigation, I represent First Municipal Bank. I am writing in response to your notice of 1 July 2016, which we received on 4 July 2016, requesting records of all correspondence between and among the officers of First Municipal Bank for the time period of 1 January 2011 to the present.

(…)

Yours sincerely
Sidney Stone

6

The following sections contain alternative formulations for certain portions of the response, allowing you to tailor your correspondence to the substance you intend to convey.

B.   Agreeing to the Request in Part

- My client intends to comply with your notice. However, …
- While we agree to provide you with the bulk of the requested documents, certain of the correspondence you requested is privileged and will, therefore, not be produced.
- Before we can produce the documents, we require a protective order/ assurances of confidentiality from you.
- While we have commenced the process of locating and retrieving the documents you requested, the timeline you proposed is unrealiztic, given …
- In your notice, you requested that we … by [date]. Unfortunately, we will not be able to comply with this deadline, because …

C.   Politely Declining to Follow the Request

- As you know, my client has been very cooperative in this investigation. However, …
- We are not in a position to provide the documents you request, as …
- We disagree with your assertion that the correspondence you requested is relevant to this investigation. To the contrary, …
- In light of the law, we believe the documents you requested are beyond the scope of this investigation. As such, we will not be producing them.
- We have already provided you with …, and do not believe that the additional documents you now request are subject to production because …
- Given the documents' extensive volume, and the nature of our client's archiving software, providing all of the documents you request is simply not possible/would place an undue burden on my client.

Practice Tip

It is helpful to emphasize your client's willingness to cooperate. Thus, if you cannot or do not intend to comply with the request or a portion of the request, do not use the phrases "we cannot comply with your request" or "we are unable to comply with the demands in your notice." Doing so may make your client appear uncooperative, even if there are legitimate grounds for the refusal to comply.

Instead, it is customary to state that your client is not able or not in a position to provide the particular items requested, e.g. "we are unable to turn over/provide you with/ locate/produce correspondence between [certain individuals]/for the time range of [date] to [date]." In addition, provide the specific facts, and – where applicable – law supporting your position.

Personal Notes _____

_____

_____

_____

_____

_____

_____

_____

_____

_____

_____

7 Template for a Research Memorandum

A Research Memorandum summarizes your research on and your legal analysis of one or more issues affecting your case. Unlike documents filed with the court, which involve persuasive writing, a Research Memorandum provides an objective, realistic analysis of the law as it applies to your case. The Research Memorandum guides your legal advice to the client, and may ultimately serve as the basis for a pleading to the court.

Research Memoranda are commonly drafted using a modified version of the IRAC Structure, which stands for (1) Issue, (2) Rule, (3) Analysis, and (4) Conclusion. This generally accepted structure is as follows:

- *Issue/Question Presented*
- *Short Answer/Executive Summary*
- *Facts*
- *Analysis/Discussion*
- *Conclusion*

Memorandum

• TO:	• [*Partner/Colleague Name*] • File
• FROM:	• [*Your name*] • [*Your position, your location (if you practice in a firm with multiple offices)*]
• DATE:	• August 31, 2016 (UK: 31 August 2016)
• RE:	• Concise statement of the research issue, e.g. "Analysis of whether §… of the Delaware Corporate Code applies to [name of your matter]"

A.   Issue/Question Presented

This section contains a concise statement, phrased as a one-sentence question, and including relevant factual information, of the issue addressed in the Memorandum. The statement of the Issue/Question Presented usually contains the key factual information relevant to the analysis.

If the Memorandum addresses multiple issues, the heading should read "Issues" (or "Questions Presented"). Each of the issues should be phrased as a separate question, and each should be in a separate paragraph under this heading.

Examples:
- Does §... of the Delaware Corporate Code apply to Blackstone's proposed acquisition of Global Health, LLC, given that Global Health LLC is a not-for-profit enterprise?
- Under what circumstances will Mr. Black's renunciation of his citizenship trigger tax consequences under IRC §...?
- Did Saran Industries comply with New York State employment law in terminating the employment of [employee name] for [reason(s)]?
- Did Snyder Telecommunications ("Snyder") breach the exclusivity provision of the licensing agreement with its supplier of wireless routers, Routers Inc. ("Routers"), by engaging in preliminary discussions with a different supplier of wireless routers in January 2016?

B.   Short Answer/Executive Summary

Where possible, the Short Answer/Executive Summary section should start with a simple "Yes" or "No," followed by a very brief explanation of the reason(s) for your answer. If you cannot provide a clear "Yes" or "No" answer, state that a certain outcome is "likely," "not likely," "unlikely," "probable," "possible," or that "there is a risk/chance that…".

For ease of readability, the language and structure of the Short Answer/ Executive Summary section should mirror the language and structure of the Issue/Question Presented.

The entire section should be no more than one short paragraph, or two very short paragraphs at the very most. It should succinctly set forth your conclusion, refer to the key facts and the relevant law, and allow the reader to understand the gist of the analysis underlying your conclusion.

Examples:

- Yes, §… of the Delaware Corporate Code applies to the proposed acquisition, as §… governs all mergers, consolidations, or conversions of corporate entities, and does not distinguish between for profit and not-for-profit enterprises.
- Although we will have to confirm several details of Mr. Black's financial situation to reach a final determination on this question, my research revealed that Mr. Black's renunciation of his citizenship is likely to trigger tax consequences if (1) his net worth exceeds …, and (2) his tax liability in the past five years has consistently exceeded …
- Based on my research, a court would most likely find that Saran Industries complied with New York State employment law when it terminated the employment of …, as …
- As the exclusivity provision of Synder's licensing agreement with Routers does not expressly prohibit Snyder from entering into preliminary discussions with other suppliers of wireless routers, and as there is no support in the law for finding that a breach occurred under these circumstances, we can make a strong argument that Snyder's did not breach the agreement.

C.   Facts

This section sets forth the facts relevant to your analysis in narrative form. The facts should be set forth in chronological order. The facts section should not include facts that do not play a role in your analysis. Where you are forced to make certain assumptions in your analysis, state those assumptions clearly.

If you are relying on certain documents in making your analysis, you can identify and cite these documents in the Facts section.

The Facts section serves a two-fold purpose. First, the Facts section provides the reader with context for the analysis. Second, the Facts section sets forth the assumptions on which your analysis relies. Making the assumptions underlying the analysis explicit is useful because it allows the author or another reader to amend the analysis more easily if the facts change, or if additional facts become known at a later point.

Examples:

- On January 31, 2015, Blackstone, a for-profit Delaware corporation, began discussions with Global Health, LLC, a not-for-profit provider of medical services listed and head-quartered in Los Angeles, California, regarding Blackstone's interest in acquiring Global Health. By March 2015, the two entities had agreed that the proposed acquisition was in both parties' interest, and executed a Letter of Intent setting forth the key terms of the acquisition (Letter of Intent, referred to below as "LOI," dated March 15, 2015). (…)

- Our client, Mr. John Black, intends to renounce his United States citizenship effective this year for personal reasons. He has asked us for advice regarding the possible tax consequences of the renunciation. A list setting forth Mr. Black's assets is attached to this Memorandum as Appendix A. For purposes of this analysis, we are assuming that Mr. Black does not currently have any outstanding tax liabilities to the US or any foreign government. (…)

- In January 2015, Saran Industries ("Saran") hired [*employee name*] as its controller in its New York office. Within the first month of his employment, [*employee name*] missed work on three occasions without obtaining prior approval. After the third of these unexcused absences from work, Saran's Human Resources department issued a written reprimand to [*employee name*] stating that the company would not tolerate further unexcused absences (see January 30, 2015 Letter to [*employee name*]). However, this letter did not make explicit what consequences, if any, [*employee name*] would suffer if he missed work again without obtaining prior approval. (…)

- In June 2015, Snyder entered into a licensing agreement with Routers, under which Snyder obtained permission to use the well-known Routers name for marketing purposes (June 1, 2015 Licensing Agreement, referred to below as the "Agreement"). The Agreement contained an exclusivity provision under which Snyder agreed not to enter into any licensing or supplier agreements with other providers of wireless routers. (*See* Agreement, § 9). (…)

7

D. Analysis/Discussion

The Analysis/Discussion section forms the main part of your Memorandum, and should follow this structure:

Umbrella paragraph: The umbrella paragraph provides a short overview of the relevant law and serves as a road map on the issues your analysis addresses, as well as the structure of your analysis.

Analysis subsections:

* Legal rule
* Explanation of the legal rule
* Application of the legal rule to the facts of your case

Examples – Legal Rule:
* Under New York State's Minimum Wage Act, codified in Art. 19 of the New York State Labor Law, all employees in New York State must receive at least $9.00 per hour of work.
* Where a court is tasked with deciding whether a party has infringed a valid patent, the court will apply a three-part test under federal law.
* Under New York state law, an employer can generally terminate an employee at any time and for any reason other than a reason in violation of public policy, unless an employee's contract or a specific law provides otherwise.

Examples – Explanation of the Legal Rule:
* This means that ...
* Courts applying this section of the statute have interpreted the language ... to mean that ...
* The three-part test which applies to patent cases contains the following elements/prongs/factors: ...
* There are, however, two exceptions to this rule. First, in cases where ... Second, if ..., the law states that ...

> **Examples – Application of the Legal Rule:**
> - Here/in this case/under these facts/in the instant situation, this means that ...
> - Applying the law to the facts, ...
> - Given our set of facts, a court would most likely apply this rule to find ...
> - The cases interpreting this provision are sufficiently similar to the facts of our case to allow the conclusion that ... For example, in [*name of case*], ..., and the court found that ... Similarly, in our case, ...

E.   Conclusion

Your Conclusion section should be very brief, ideally no more than one or two sentences, and no longer than four sentences at the most. The Conclusion simply states your overall findings on each of the issues addressed in your Memorandum. The Conclusion should not contain any new facts, issues, or arguments that you have not discussed in the Memorandum.

> **Examples – Conclusion:**
> - In conclusion, I believe, based on my research, that we can argue ...
> - It is, thus, likely/unlikely/probable/very probable that ...
> - We can/should, therefore, advise [*client name*] that ...
> - In light of the foregoing, there is a risk/chance/low probability/ high probability that a court will find that ...

8 Contract Drafting

A. Introduction to Contract Drafting

This section discusses basic contract drafting principles and language. You can use it to critically edit and assess your approach to drafting and reviewing contracts and contract templates.

Lawyers across different practice areas and in practically every industry are increasingly drafting, reviewing, and negotiating contracts in English. Such contracts can include diverse documents setting out obligations and rights (e.g. share-purchase agreements). As contracts deal with future events and possibilities, they are by their nature adversarial and technical.

In addition, legal culture plays an important role in contract drafting. When dealing with international business contracts, lawyers must understand the native culture of drafting in other jurisdictions.

Effective legal drafting involves setting out as clearly as possible the parties' rights and duties. This chapter's purpose is to provide some useful tips for lawyers to achieve additional clarity in drafting contracts.

Key Concepts in Contracts

Contract Formation
- A contract is an agreement that is *binding upon* and *legally enforceable against* the contracting parties. Under common law, a contract must meet the following essential elements to be binding:
  – Offer
  – Acceptance
  – Consideration
  – Meeting of the Minds
- A contract is *entered into/created* when one party *makes an offer* which the other party accepts without proposing any additional or alternative terms or conditions. The term "to conclude a contract" is ambiguous, and drafters should avoid it in favor of "entered into" or "created." A counter-offer (i.e. a new offer that changes the terms of the original offer) does not constitute acceptance. Acceptance can occur orally, in writing, or through performance.

- *Consideration* is defined in the common law as *a bargained-for exchange of value that the parties are not otherwise required to provide.* Often, consideration is the purchase price, but it need not be money. It can be something else of value that induces the agreement, e.g. performance of a service, waiver of a right, or forbearance with regard to taking action which the party would otherwise be entitled to take. A mere promise by one party to do something without any consideration by the other party is not a contract, and therefore not enforceable under contract law, nor is a gift. This distinction, hinging on consideration as a requirement to enforceability, is a notable difference between contracts under the common law and contracts under certain civil law regimes.
- *Meeting of the Minds* means that the parties agree on the terms of their contract, and are not mistaken or misinformed about the terms at issue.

Performance of the Contract

In addition to choosing the correct language in a contract, the contract drafter must also understand the types of contract provisions, how they work, and how they allocate risk between the parties. Obligations arising from a contract or agreement are usually found in the main section of the contract. Whenever a contract creates a duty, the contract also grants a corresponding right to the party who has an interest in the performance of the obligation by the promisor. If one party breaches a duty, the injured party may be entitled to a remedy (for example, compensatory damages, injunctive relief, or specific performance). In addition, where a court finds a breach to be "material," the court may excuse the non-breaching party from performing its obligations under the contract.

Other Key Concepts

- A *covenant* (used as a noun and verb) involves a promise to do or refrain from doing something in a contract. One party promises (covenants) to do or not do something, creating an obligation, while the other party thereby receives a corresponding right. Contracts typically contain multiple covenants. In common law contracts, covenants, like any obligation, are enforceable only if adequate consideration exists. Contracts typically express covenants using the verbs "must" and "will." *Example:* The company *must* deliver the Goods, as defined herein, within one month of the order date.

217

- A *condition* is a requirement which must be met for the contractual obligation(s) to be enforceable. Meeting the requirement may create or terminate an obligation or right. A *condition precedent* expresses what must happen before a contractual obligation becomes enforceable, while a *condition subsequent* sets forth what must happen in order for a contractual obligation to be terminated. Contracts typically express conditions using phrases such as "if," "if and only if," "if…, then," "in the event that," or "on the condition that."
  Example: If the Company notifies the Supplier of any defect within 18 days, then the Supplier must replace the rejected Machinery.
- Contracts often contain sections dealing jointly with both *representations* and *warranties.*
- A *representation* is a statement of fact (not an opinion, statement of intention, or a statement relating to a future event) a party makes prior to or at the time of entering into the contract. It is made with the intention to influence the other party to act, i.e. to enter into the contract. Courts examine the truthfulness of representations at the time they were made. If one party's representation turns out to be false (i.e., a misrepresentation), the other party may, in many cases, if the misrepresentation induced the party to enter into the contract, be able to bring a claim for damages or rescission.
  Example of a representation: The company represents that it has a full and unlimited right to provide the Services.
- A *warranty,* by contrast, involves a statement of future performance or quality of services or products. If that statement turns out to be false, the other party may have a claim for breach of warranty giving rise to a damages claim. Warranties can be either express or implied (the law may imply or expressly provide for warranties in specific sectors or industries).
  Example of warranty: The company warrants that all delivered goods will be of the same quality as the delivered sample.

B.   Preparing a Draft Contract

This section discusses key considerations of which you should be aware before you start drafting a contract.

A contract involves an exchange relationship created by an oral or written agreement between two or more parties. Contracts can be bilateral (between two parties) or multilateral (among three or more parties). Under common law, a valid contract involves mutual obligations which the law recognizes as enforceable. As a result, effective contract drafting requires that you understand the parties' goals and the potential situations that the contract must cover.

Before you can commence with your first draft, make sure you understand the purpose of the agreement. Start by creating an outline of the contract, and break it down into smaller parts or sections. Doing so helps to ensure that the contract covers all the intended issues and that it is organized in a logical manner. It is common practice to insert boilerplate clauses (industry standard clauses requiring little to no negotiation) into your outline as a placeholder pending the contract negotiations' outcome. These are commonly inserted in square brackets ([…]) so that the parties can easily find and amend them at a later stage.

Effective contract drafting requires that you revise and edit your initial draft before using it in practice. To this end, use a multi-phase approach to editing, and revise your document after (not while) you complete your first draft. Doing so helps you to focus on particular writing issues, e.g. paragraph structure, or consistency within the document as a whole. Critically review each word, phrase, sentence, and paragraph to assess its accuracy and its importance to the document as a whole.

a.   *Background Information*

To ensure that the draft contract covers all the issues the parties intend to address, lawyers have to obtain all the relevant and necessary instructions and information from the client in advance of creating a first draft. To tailor your draft to the client's needs, spend sufficient time with the client discussing the initial instructions. Often, such discussions will reveal new information that the client's initial instructions had not addressed. In addition, where possible, review similar case files in your office to better understand the client's position. Then, create a list of issues that you will address with the client. For clients outside of your jurisdiction (and especially non-lawyers), make sure that the client understands the legal terminology you use and the extent to which it may differ from the client's legal system. Consider factors outside of the agreement that may affect how the client would like you to draft the contract (for example, current industry recommendations or drafting trends).

b.   Negotiation

You may have to draft and agree on a business term sheet providing general negotiation terms before drafting the full contract and negotiating the final terms and legal aspects. In the interest of time, lawyers may choose to leave more contentious issues aside while negotiating other issues on which finding an agreement requires less upfront effort. With the less contentious issues out of the way, parties may be more open to compromise.

After preparing the term sheet, the parties will negotiate the final contract. The lawyer who drafted the contract will often forward the final draft to opposing counsel. After reviewing the draft, opposing counsel will raise any points of contention and propose solutions. At this point, lawyers will help their clients decide on which proposed changes to the contract they may be willing to compromise, and which issues may be non-negotiable.

Drafting Tip

The negotiation process takes time. In some situations, lawyers will draw up a "letter of intent" (LOI) or "memorandum of understanding" (MOU) before the contract is final. An LOI or MOU involves a statement from the parties outlining their intent to enter into a contract on certain terms. However, note that while such preliminary documents are not intended to be binding on the parties, courts in various jurisdictions have found that such a statement may constitute a contract, even where there is express wording to the contrary. Therefore, take care to state in the LOI or MOU itself, as well as in accompanying correspondence, that the document is preliminary and non-binding. In addition, leave at least one material term, such as cost, price, amount, or delivery date open, as documents lacking an agreement on a material term tend to be deemed non-binding.

c.   *The Law*

Carefully research the applicable law, and be aware of custom, policy, and compliance considerations before creating a first draft, In general, modern contract law seeks to facilitate trade and regulate business transactions. The law will often – but not always – seek to protect the rights of parties in a weaker bargaining position, for example consumers and employees.

By way of example, if any doubt exists regarding the enforceability of the agreement, make sure to bring such doubts to the client's attention before you start drafting the contract.

> **Examples of custom**
> While contract interpretation will vary among jurisdictions, the following list addresses some common law contract interpretation guidelines of which you should be aware. Courts in common law jurisdictions often:
> - in interpreting a contract, decline to consider any evidence, such as prior communications, memoranda, or earlier drafts of an agreement, outside of the agreement itself (known as the "four-corner" rule), unless the parties can establish conclusively that a particular term or provision is ambiguous (known as the "parol evidence rule" or PER);
> - find against a party seeking to rely on an ambiguous provision, particularly when this party drafted the contract or the provision at issue (known as the "contra preferendum" rule);
> - find that an ambiguous provision should be interpreted so as to harmonize it with other provisions in the contract;
> - prefer an interpretation of a contract that renders the whole contract enforceable rather than voiding certain provisions (known as the "whole contract" rule);
> - give preference to specific over general terms ("specific over general terms" rule);
> - find that words should be given their ordinary meaning ("ordinary meaning" rule); and
> - if terms or provisions are ambiguous, analyze the parties' course of dealing in order to establish what they intended under the contract (the "course of dealing" rule).

d.   Your Audience

For effective drafting, consider who will read the contract in the future. Contracts are often targeted at legal professionals, including judges and the opposing lawyers. However, be aware that the contract will also be read by the clients, their employees, agents, and other third parties, as well as, potentially, parties outside your jurisdiction.

Consequently, choose clear and simple language that lawyers and non-lawyers can understand equally well, as well as stand-alone terms that do not require additional context or interpretation.

> **Drafting Tip**
> In many cases, foreign legal terms or concepts will not have equivalent terminology in the target language. Research how best to describe legal concepts expressed in the source language. You may have to decipher the source language and reconstruct its meaning in the target language. Lawyers commonly define or describe legal terminology in the source language which has no equivalent wording in the target language.
>
> You may also choose to "borrow" legal terminology from other jurisdictions to explain a foreign concept. This means that the drafter consciously uses the same word in the target document as is used in the source document.
>
> In each of the above situations, the terms you choose must clearly reflect the parties' intentions under the contract.

e.   The Draft

Carefully consider who will create the first draft, as the drafter will often establish the conditions for the contract negotiations that follow. In addition, the drafter who prepares the first version of the contract's terms will be more familiar with the individual contract provisions.

The contract must state the business position between the parties accurately. Therefore, keep the contract in line with the client's instructions. Changing or inserting new terms or provisions without authority from your client to do so can create disagreements between or among the parties and the lawyers, may be considered unethical, and may even constitute malpractice.

Lawyers often rely on precedents (also known as contract models or templates) when drafting contracts. Be aware that over-relying on templates poses a substantial risk in contract drafting. When you use precedents, review them very carefully to ensure that they are appropriate for the particular transaction. In cross-border transactions, precedent from one legal jurisdiction may be inappropriate for use in another. Make sure your draft excludes all unnecessary clauses and wording included in any precedent on which you rely. Inadvertently leaving inapplicable precedent clauses in a draft may lead to disagreements between parties, as the non-drafting party might view such oversights as a unilateral attempt to obtain a more favorable position under the contract.

> **Drafting Tip**
>
> If you are drafting a contract still under negotiation, place the relevant sections (including any relevant precedent clauses) in brackets ([…]) pending the outcome of the negotiations. Place any boilerplate clauses (industry standard clauses) in brackets ([…]) until all parties are fully satisfied with the chosen wording.

f.   Interpretation Issues

Contract drafting pitfalls can arise when parties do not clearly set out their intentions or expectations. Common issues include vagueness and ambiguity with respect to aspects of the contract. Other issues can involve key terms that are omitted or remain unresolved and non-binding despite extensive negotiation. Such issues can result in disputes, litigation, and a contract's unenforceability.

In some jurisdictions, courts may imply standard terms based on the law, regulations, or public policy considerations into contracts to clarify a contract's wording and give effect to the parties' intentions. A contractual agreement to exclude, narrow, or circumvent such terms is often unenforceable.

This section provides two key drafting tips to avoid disputes about a contract's language, and to avoid requiring judicial intervention to interpret a contract.

8

Drafting Tip – Avoid Ambiguity

Ambiguity occurs where words or phrases create conflicting meanings or are subject to different reasonable interpretations. Ambiguous terms often lead the parties to ask for judicial assistance in interpreting the contract, which can quickly get costly and adversarial. To avoid ambiguity:

- Be aware that using multiple terms for the same meaning can cause ambiguity. Be consistent throughout the document, ensuring that the language in the precedent clause matches the language of your draft (e.g. if the precedent uses "agreement," avoid using "contract"). Do not use one term to refer to multiple parties or events. Conversely, use precisely the same, rather than multiple different terms, to refer to a single party, person, or event. For complex contracts, consider inserting a Definitions section.
- Be careful not to express the same concept differently throughout the contract. Follow the same format, e.g. do not use "reasonable care" in one part of the contract and "due care and diligence" in another, if you mean the same thing.
- Be careful when using pronouns. Pronouns, particularly "it" and "they," can give rise to ambiguity if a sentence or short paragraph includes multiple nouns to which the pronoun could reasonably refer. If using a pronoun could give rise to ambiguity, replace the pronoun with a noun.
- Write out dates if their format could give rise to ambiguity (i.e. if a US reader and a European reader would interpret a date, such as 5/7/2016 differently).
- Apply the Plain Language rules.
- Carefully follow English grammar and punctuation rules, and budget sufficient time for careful editing.
- Check your draft for consistency among various different parts of your contract. While focusing on specific words and paragraphs, you may have missed inconsistencies in wording among the contract's provisions that could give rise to ambiguity.

Drafting Tip – Avoid Vagueness

Vagueness can result from using words or phrases in an uncertain or obscure manner so that their intended meaning is unclear, e.g. when words or phrases have a particular meaning, but questions remain regarding their scope.

Examples of commonly used but risky terms in contract drafting include "reasonable," "best efforts," and "material damage." These terms may sound clear, but interpreting and fulfilling them can, in practice, easily give rise to disputes and even litigation. Consequently, avoid such terms if possible. Alternatively, try to define or narrow such vague terms by using examples (e.g. "best efforts including but not limited to actions such as [...]").

Personal Notes _____

_____

_____

_____

_____

_____

_____

_____

_____

_____

_____

_____

225

8

g. *Main Sections of the Contract*

The following section lists common components of common law contracts. Use it for reference in the drafting process or in reviewing an existing contract.

Heading(s)	Headings are placed in the center of the contract's first page, usually in a larger bold typeface. The heading should identify the contract's nature as much as possible (e.g. International Agency Agreement). Note that the heading commonly employs the term "agreement" rather than "contract" although both terms are synonymous.
Contracting parties	The contract's introductory statement, which comes directly after the heading, identifies the parties to the contract and their correct legal description (whether they are natural persons, partnerships, companies etc.). To make sure you use a party's correct legal name, carefully research the parties' accurate descriptions under the applicable law. Include the parties' addresses in their description and use the words "between" (for two parties) or "among" (for more than two parties) to describe the parties' contractual relationship. It is common to shorten the parties' names in the introductory statement by using defined terms, e.g. Saran Industries ("Saran") or Jack Black (the "Contractor"). Always ensure that defined terms are capitalized and used in a consistent manner throughout the text.

Contract date	The contract date is commonly included in the introductory statement or at the end of the contract. The language in the introductory statement may vary as a result, i.e. "This contract entered into between …" or "This Contract dated …" The execution date (when the parties sign the contract) is frequently but not always the contract's effective date (when the contract comes into force). In some cases, however, the contract will have separate execution and effective dates. In such cases, the contract's core provisions should include a clause to this effect (e.g. "the Effective Date shall be ten calendar days after the date on which all parties have executed the contract").
Recitals	After the introductory statement, some contracts contain recitals providing the reader with information concerning the contract (e.g. the parties' intentions or the most important background facts). The recitals should not include substantive terms of the contract. It is now common practice in modern contracts to use the headings "Recitals" or "Background Facts."
Transitional clause	The transitional clause follows the recitals and makes clear to the reader that the recitals are finished and the readers will now move to the next stage of the contract (e.g. "The parties agree as follows: […]").
Main provisions	This section of the contract deals with the parties' rights and obligations under the contract, and commonly includes terms dealing with consideration, the goods or services at issue, performance, term and termination, and compensation under the contract. The type and number of provisions will vary depending on the nature of the contract.
Execution page	The end of the contract includes the parties' signatures and the date of execution. (Again, be careful to distinguish this from the effective date if necessary). Any appendices, for instance definitions or timelines, are usually included in schedules after the execution page.

8

C.   Contract Structure

This section discusses how to structure a contract effectively to promote clarity and precision. First, make it easy for your audience to locate the most important terms. To increase readability, front-load the contract so that the most important information and key provisions are near the beginning. Second, use headings and numbering, both of which are vital to structuring a contract efficiently.

The following sections set out the typical structure of an international commercial contract. The example below involves a contract on consulting services, but can be adapted to numerous other scenarios.

a.   *Introductory Section*

At the outset, a contract sets out the nature of the agreement and identifies the contracting parties in detail. It commonly commences with a heading identifying the type of contract in question. The next sections identify the parties and provide the contract's effective date. Depending on the contract, this first portion of the contract may also include recitals and a transitional clause.

Drafting Tips – Introductory Section

The title should address the nature of the agreement, e.g. Agreement for Services, Purchase Agreement, Purchase and Sale Agreement, Merger Agreement, Employment Agreement, Licensing Agreement, Nondisclosure Agreement.

Make sure you know the parties' full names and descriptions before entering into a contract, i.e. whether they are natural persons, companies, partnerships, or sole proprietors, as well as where they reside (for natural persons) or where their principal place of business is located (for corporate entities). As identifying the correct legal name can be difficult, research each party's accurate description under the applicable law. It is common to include the parties' addresses in their description. Consider shortening the parties' names in the introductory statement by using defined terms, e.g. Saran Industries ("Saran") or Jack Black (the "Contractor").

The contract date is generally the date on which the parties execute the contract. Reference this date in the introductory statement or at the end of the contract (e.g. "This contract entered into between …" or "This Contract dated …"). The execution date is usually but not always also the contract's effective date (i.e. the date the contract takes effect). In some cases, however, the contract may have separate execution and effective dates. In such cases, include a clause to this effect (e.g. "The contract's Effective Date shall be ten calendar days after the date on which all parties have executed the contract.")

The agreement itself, the parties, any relevant locations, any work to be performed, and the effective date should all be defined terms, which will be used consistently throughout the rest of the contract with no variation whatsoever. Always ensure that defined terms are capitalized and used consistently throughout the document.

Example – Introductory Section

AGREEMENT FOR SERVICES

This Agreement for Services (the "Agreement") is entered into between Party A LIMITED, a company incorporated under the laws of the State of Delaware under registration number 1234567 and having its registered office at [Address] (the "Company") and Party B, an individual residing at [Address] (the "Consultant"), collectively referred to herein as the "Parties" and individually as a "Party."

b.   Definitions

Definitions provide clarity, especially in long contracts. They help to avoid ambiguity where a word or phrase may be susceptible to more than one interpretation, or to shorten a long description in a contract for ease of readability.

A good definition should be as short as possible and as long as necessary, to reflect the parties' exact intentions as to the term defined. The first letter of the defined term should be capitalized each time it is used in the contract.

Definitions are commonly inserted at the beginning of a contract, but can also be in a separate Definitions section, depending on your drafting style and the number of definitions. Longer contracts typically feature a separate schedule for definitions.

Example – Definitions

Definitions

For purposes of this Agreement, the following words and expressions mean:

- "Agreement" means the agreement between the Parties for performance of the Services.
- "Compensation" means the fees payable to the Consultant by the Company for the performance of the Services, as defined herein.
- "Services" means the Services to be performed by the Consultant for the Company as described in Schedule A.
- "Term" means the duration of the Agreement as set out in Clause 8.

---

c. Recitals

Recitals are optional, but are useful to provide additional context on background facts, the parties' intentions, or important documentation.

You can start the Recitals using the traditional term "Whereas," or you may choose more straightforward headings such as "Recitals," "Background Facts," or even a simple statement such as: "This contract is entered into under the following facts:…" While recitals are not typically binding in nature, courts may use them to establish the parties' true intentions.

If you use recitals in a contract, include a transitional clause to signal the end of the recitals and the beginning of the contract's binding terms. The transitional clause in a common law contract should state unequivocally that both parties acknowledge (1) that consideration exists, (2) that the consideration is sufficient, and (3) that the parties have received it or will receive it under the agreement (see common wording of a transitional clause in the Example below, p. 231.)

As consideration is one of the essential elements required for a binding contract under common law, stating unequivocally that consideration exists helps guarantee that the contract cannot later be deemed void for lack of consideration. Drafters unfamiliar with US law might be tempted to omit this sentence, but in doing so, would be doing their clients a great disservice and potentially exposing the contract to enforceability challenges.

Example – Recitals and Transitional clause

Recitals
The Consultant offers Consulting Services in the area of [...]. The Company wishes to retain the Consulting Services, and the Consultant agrees to perform the Consulting Services for the Company for the period of time and the consideration specified in this Agreement.

Transitional clause
In consideration of the foregoing and of the covenants and agreements contained herein, and other good and valuable consideration, the receipt and sufficiency of which are hereby acknowledged, the Parties hereby agree as follows: [...]

---

d.   *Body of the Contract*

The body of the contract deals with the parties' core rights and obligations under the contract. As this part of the contract sets out the main details of performance under the contract, it will depend on the nature of the parties' agreement. All material terms must be sufficiently definite to avoid ambiguity, and must, of course, relate solely to legal activity.

Material Terms

To be binding, a contract should include *at least* the following material terms:

(1) *Description of the specific goods or services at issue:* for goods, this term should include information on quantity and quality, where applicable.

(2) *Consideration:* this term should specify the nature and amount of consideration, i.e. the details on costs or price, as well as payment methods and deadlines.

(3) *Delivery conditions:* this term should include details on the relevant dates or deadlines for delivery (for goods) or performance (for services).

(4) *Contract term:* this term should specify whether the contract expires naturally after a given period of time, or whether the parties intend the contract to continue indefinitely absent a breach. The section should also address whether, when, and how the parties can extend or renew an initial term for one or more subsequent terms.

Common terms:

Common law contracts generally also contain many of the following provisions:

(5) *Termination:* this term should specify the grounds for termination of the contract, as well as any conditions precedent to termination, notice procedures, and any deadlines or notice periods for termination. Contracts may also include a right of termination in the event of specific situations, e.g. in the case of an insolvency or change in control of one of the parties.

(6) *Dispute resolution:* this term should specify whether the parties, in the event of a future dispute, agree to resolve the dispute through litigation or through an alternative form of dispute resolution, e.g. arbitration or mediation.

(7) *Jurisdiction and Venue:* this term should specify which court or other tribunal has jurisdiction over disputes arising from the contract, and in which forum the parties agree to bring any such disputes.

(8) *Governing Law:* this term should specify which law(s) or rules will be used to interpret the contract, i.e. the law of a particular state, country, or other set of rules. Note that while the parties are free to choose the governing law of a contract, the decision on whether the choice of law provision is enforceable will be made in the court where the suit is brought.

(9) *Indemnification:* this term involves a duty on one party, under certain circumstances, to pay for financial losses of another relating to the contract, work performed thereunder, or goods provided thereunder. It may also involve a duty to defend the other party from third-party claims related to the contract.

(10) *Severability:* this term should specify what will happen to the remaining contract if a court finds a specific provision unenforceable. Including a severability clause will help avoid invalidating an entire contract based on the invalidity of one con-tract provision.

(11) *Damages:* it is not necessary to insert a term specifying the amount of damages in the event of a breach, and the parties may leave the matter of damages to the courts. However, the parties may address the types of damages (as well as other remedies) available in the contract in the event of a breach. Under common law, such damages may include consequential damages (damages flowing from the breach), as well as damages which are incidental (indirect or arising when dealing with the breach).

(12) *Liquidated Damages:* a liquidated damages clause specifies, in advance, the amount of damages payable in the event of a breach. To be enforceable, a liquidated damages clause must be non-punitive, and must be reasonably based on the non-breaching party's economic loss.

(13) *Limitation of liability:* this term should set out any limits on which the parties have agreed regarding the conduct for which a party may be liable and the type or amount of damages available in the event of a breach.

(14) *Force Majeure:* this term should specify any events that will forgive non-performance by a party of a contractual obligation. In general, non-performance will only be forgiven where the event is defined in the Force Majeure clause.

(15) *Merger Clause:* this term provides that the agreement at issue is the complete and final agreement between or among the parties, and that no documents other than those included in, attached to, or incorporated by reference are part of the agreement. Common law courts generally interpret the merger clause to mean that no terms, conditions, or implied considerations apply other than those set forth in the agreement.

(16) *Counterparts:* where the parties are not in the same place to sign a contract, this term can specify that the contract can be executed in counterparts, and that e-mailed and faxed signatures are valid.

(17) *Taxes:* this term typically mandates that a party is responsible for paying his or her own taxes.

(18) *Non-Competition Clause:* this term restricts individuals and organizations from providing certain services or engaging in certain businesses in certain markets and geographic areas for a period of time. The enforceability of such clauses varies significantly among jurisdictions.

Body of the Contract – Sample Clauses

You can use the following examples of common contract clauses for reference when drafting new contract provisions. The purpose of these sample provisions, together with the other information in this chapter, is to provide you with information on typical contract language and ideas for creating your own set of precedent clauses. Note that terms such as "parties" or "agreement," which are generally capitalized, are not capitalized in the examples below. This choice is deliberate, **as these examples should not be viewed as model precedents. Each transaction and each contract is unique and requires careful, customized drafting based on the applicable facts and the contract's governing law.**

Term of the Agreement

This agreement will become effective when both parties sign it, and will remain in effect for one year from the effective date unless otherwise terminated pursuant to this agreement by notice of termination, as specifically set forth in […]

Termination

Either party may terminate this agreement upon written notice to the other, if the other party breaches any material obligation and fails to cure the breach within thirty days.

Method of Notice

A party wishing to terminate the agreement must communicate the termination to the other party, by written notice of termination, in accordance with the provisions set forth in the notices section.

Definition of "Notice of Termination"

For purposes of this agreement, a "Notice of Termination" means a notice which indicates the specific termination provision in this agreement on which the terminating party relies, and sets forth in reasonable detail the facts and circumstances claimed to provide a basis for termination as set forth in […] of this agreement.

Alternative Dispute Resolution (ADR)

The parties agree that any dispute or controversy, arising out of or in connection with this Agreement or any alleged breach thereof, shall be fully and finally resolved by final and binding arbitration administered by National Arbitration and Mediation ("NAM") in accordance with NAM's Comprehensive Dispute Resolution Rules and Procedures and the Fee Schedule in effect at the time the claim is filed with NAM. Any award of the arbitrator(s) is final and binding, and may be entered as a judgment in any court of competent jurisdiction.

Jurisdiction and Venue

The parties agree to submit any action at law, suit in equity, or judicial proceeding arising directly, indirectly, or otherwise in connection with, out of, related to or from this agreement, to the exclusive jurisdiction of the courts of the State of [Forum].

Governing Law

The agreement and any disputes arising thereunder or related thereto will be construed in accordance with the laws of [insert jurisdiction].

Indemnification

Party A agrees to indemnify Party B and its officers, directors, employees and agents, from and against all claims, liabilities, losses, costs, damages, judgments, penalties, fines, attorneys' fees, court costs and other legal expenses, insurance deductibles and all other expenses arising out of or relating to, directly or indirectly: the negligent, grossly negligent, or intentional act or omission of Party A or its directors, officers, employees, or agents; Party A's failure to perform any of its obligations under this agreement; and any act or omission of Party A in connection with the Work, as defined herein.

Notice of Claim

Party B will promptly notify Party A of any claim for indemnification.

Severability

The provisions in this agreement are distinct and severable. If any provision, or part of a provision is found to be invalid, unenforceable, illegal, or void by a court or other authority, such provision or part of a provision shall be deemed not part of the agreement, and the validity, enforceability, and legality of the remainder of the agreement will not be affected.

Liquidated Damages

In the event of a breach of contract by Party A, Party A will pay liquidated damages to Party B at a rate of [$...]. Such liquidated damages shall be deemed to be a reasonable, foreseeable, and genuine estimate of Party B's economic loss resulting from the breach of contract by Party A.

Limitation of Liability

Party B will not be liable to Party A in excess of the compensation paid to Party B under this agreement, or in excess of the sum of [$...] whichever is greater. Party B's liability under this agreement is limited to instances where Party A proves that the act or omission amounting to a breach of contract was committed in a willful or intentional manner.

Force Majeure

Neither party will be in breach of this agreement for any delay in performance or non-performance of obligations under this agreement if that delay or non-performance is due to Force Majeure, as that term is defined in this agreement.

Entire Agreement

This agreement contains the entire agreement of the parties, and there are no other promises or conditions in any other agreement, whether oral or written.

Counterparts

The agreement may be executed in two (2) counterparts, each of which shall be deemed an original, and both of which together constitute one and the same document.

Taxes

Party A will not be responsible for any tax-related or other legal obligations applicable to Party B.

Non-Competition Clause

Party A agrees that, both during the term of this agreement and for a period of 6 months thereafter, Party A will not provide services to, or enter into any agreements with, any competitor of Party B in the greater Los Angeles area.

e.   *Execution Page*

The end of the contract includes the parties' signatures and the date of execution. Any appendices, for instance definitions or timelines, are usually included in schedules after the signatures.

Example

IN WITNESS whereof the parties have entered into this agreement this [Date] day of [Month], [Year].

For and on behalf of
Party A LIMITED

_____   _____
Date   By:
                           Its:

For and on behalf of
Party B LIMITED

_____   _____
Date   By:
                           Its:

D.   Language in Contracts

This section discusses the advantages and pitfalls of common contract language. Use it to critically assess and edit contracts after your initial draft(s) and to ensure effective communication with your audience.

Plain Legal English

In drafting contracts, lawyers often rely on precedent, i.e. templates or similar contracts that they or others have prepared for use in other transactions. Such precedent can contain unnecessarily complicated "legalese" that is incomprehensible to non-lawyers. The Plain English movement suggests avoiding legalese in favor of simpler language so that lawyers and non-lawyers alike can more readily understand legal documents. As the movement toward Plain English in professional drafting is gaining steam across different jurisdictions, consider substituting Plain English for formal and technical language in contracts.

While re-drafting contracts to simplify their structure and replacing legalese with Plain English has its advantages, such re-drafting requires great care and attention to detail. When using Plain English, make sure that the terms you use are accurate and appropriately convey the precise legal meaning you intend to convey.

The following section provides professional tips and examples on how to use Plain English in the contract drafting setting. To review additional hallmarks of professional legal writing, see Part II, Chapter 1, Professional Legal Writing – Language and Style, pp. 174–181.

(1) Brevity

Sentences should be short (no more than 15–20 words). Where possible, use the parties' real names, e.g. write "Saran Industries" rather than "Mortgagor," "Buyer," or "Manufacturer."

(2) Active voice

Writing in the active voice makes contracts more accessible and helps to avoid ambiguity. The active voice often also makes sentences simpler and shorter.

Example:

Passive	Active
The goods will be delivered by the distributor to the company within 21 days of the order.	The distributor will deliver the goods to the company within 21 days of the order.

(3) Sentence Structure

Sentences are clearer when the subject, verb, and object appear together at the start of the sentence. Consider splitting long sentences containing numerous qualifications or conditions.

Example:

"The Company (subject) *by the first working day of next month* agrees to make (verb) delivery (object)"

Change to:

"The Company (subject) agrees to make (verb) delivery (object) *by the first working day of next month*"

(4) Verbs in contracts

Choosing the correct verb is essential to avoid ambiguity, although using a particular verb will not guarantee that a court will interpret a provision in a certain way. Carefully assess and differentiate among terms such as "must," "may," "must not," "may not," "need not," and "will" to ensure that the verb you choose represents what you intend the provision to mean.

Examples:
To create an obligation: *must/will.*
"The Company must provide written notice within 14 days."

To create an option or reference a possibility: *may.*
"Either party may amend the written agreement with prior written consent of the other."

To create a prohibition: *may not/shall not have the right to.*
"During the Contract Term the parties may not/shall not have the right to enter into negotiations with other suppliers."

To create a non-binding recommendation: *should.*
"Both parties should stay informed of the latest industry trends."

Drafting Tip:

Avoid using the term *"shall,"* as it can be subject to numerous interpretations. While most lawyers would agree that the term is mandatory, creating an obligation, courts have also interpreted "shall" to be permissive, meaning "may" or "should." To reference a mandatory obligation, use an unambiguous term such as "must," "will," or "has a duty to."

(5) Contractions

Avoid contractions in contracts (such as it's, doesn't, don't).

(6) Positive form

Generally, it is preferable to state terms positively, e.g. write "must be at least 15 days" rather than "no less than 15 days."

Legal Practice
Manuals for Oral Communication

1 Oral Advocacy – Phrases and Expressions

A. General Terminology for Court Proceedings

a. Bringing a case to court

- to sue someone for ...
- to bring/file a lawsuit/an action for ...
- to file a complaint seeking ...
- to take someone to court for ...
- to lodge an action against someone seeking damages for ...
- to lodge a claim against someone (UK)
- to file/lodge (UK) counterclaims
- to file an appeal in the matter of [*party name*] v. [*party name*]

b. Filing documents

- to file a pleading/motion with the court
- to submit evidence/a pleading/a motion to the court

c. Court procedure: actions by the parties

- the parties appear before the court
- counsel appears on behalf of [*client's name*]
- to deliver an opening statement
- to put on/present/submit evidence
- to read evidence into the record (US)
- to put on/call witnesses to give testimony
- to submit witness statements (UK)
- to conduct a direct examination/cross-examination of a witness (US)
- to put forth an argument/a defense
- to deliver a closing statement

d.   Court procedure: actions by the court

- to hold a hearing/proceedings/a trial on ... (US)
- to hear a case/evidence/an argument on ...
- to rule on a motion/an issue
- to grant a motion/a request by a party to ...
- to deny a motion/a request to ...
- to refuse a request for ...
- to admit/refuse to admit ... into evidence
- to strike a statement/evidence from the record
- to reject an argument
- to sustain an objection to ...
- to overrule an objection to ...
- to dismiss a claim/an action/a case/a complaint
- to issue a judgment/decision/ruling/verdict/order in favor of a party
- to render a decision on the issue of ...
- to deliver/return a verdict that ...
- to hold in favor of a party
- to award costs/attorneys' fees to a party
- to remit/remand a case to the lower court
- to allow an appeal
- to grant certiorari (US Supreme Court)

e.   Settlement

- to settle a case
- to settle out of court
- to reach a settlement
- to reach an extrajudicial resolution
- to submit a consent order to the court

f.   Referring to legal propositions

- the law states/provides/requires that ...
- the relevant case law/precedent states/provides/requires that ...
- prior court decisions on this issue have found that ...
- the Code of Obligations/statute/regulations/ordinances state(s) that ...
- Note: the term "jurisprudence" refers to a legal philosophy generally, not to case law or specific court decisions

243

g.   *Addressing or referring to others*

aa)   The court/arbitral panel

- Sir/Madam (UK)
- UK Court of Appeal and Supreme Court: My Lord (vocative, e.g. "yes, my Lord")/Your Lordship (third singular, e.g. "your Lordship may find that …")
- Your Honour (UK)/Your Honor (US)
- The Court (e.g. "The Court may find that …")
- Dear Mr. (UK: Mr)/Madame Chairman/chairperson and members of the panel

bb)   Your opponent

- my learned/esteemed friend (UK)
- my colleague (UK)
- my opponent/my adversary
- the plaintiff/the defendant
- the other side (very informal, sets a confrontational tone)

B.   The Language of Advocacy

a.   *Introduction*

- My name is …, and I am counsel for …
- I am appearing today on behalf of …
- At counsel's table/with me here today is/are my associate [*name*]/ my paralegal [*name*]/my client [*name*]
- For appeals: May it please the court, my name is …

b.   *Making your case*

aa)   Opening statement

- This matter comes before you as …
- In this matter, the court is called upon to/must decide/assess/ determine …
- The legal issue in this case is whether …
- This is a lawsuit about …
- The claimant/plaintiff submits/contends/argues/asserts/alleges/claims that …

- As you will see, the law/the facts/the evidence support(s) our case/our view/our position that …
- We will put on/put forth/introduce evidence to show that …
- I will demonstrate that the following elements of the claim are established: …
- We respectfully submit that …
- We ask/invite the court to find that …

bb) Arguing your case

- The evidence shows/establishes/demonstrates that …
- It is clear from the evidence that …
- In light of the law, the evidence allows this court to conclude/find/determine that …
- There is significant/substantial/strong/overwhelming evidence supporting our position that …
- Under the law, the evidence makes clear that my client acted correctly/did not breach the contract/fulfillled all of his obligations/met the legal standard …
- My opponent/the plaintiff/the defendant has already admitted/conceded that …
- My opponent cites [legal precedent] in support of his claim that …
- However, that [legal precedent] is distinguishable, because …

cc) Referring to legal precedent

- The law is in my client's favor, as …
- The case I have just referred you to is analogous to the instant case, in that both cases …
- There is a precedent stating that … (US)
- In the case [legal precedent] the court found that …

c. *Disagreeing with your opponent*

- Contrary to the plaintiff's/claimant's statement that …, it is in fact the case that …
- While the plaintiff/claimant would have the court believe that …, it is our position that …
- My opponent has misstated the facts/the law on …
- My opponent has overlooked the fact that …

- I disagree with my opponent's statement/view that…
- While I agree with my opponent that the law states …, applying the law to this case leads to a result different from that my opponent advocates.
- The law does not support my opponent's assertion/claim that…
- To the contrary, the law provides that…

1

2 Negotiation – Phrases and Expressions

A. Explaining your Position

a. Setting forth your position

- Our client's position/view is …
- Our goal is to …
- What we are looking for is …
- I'd like to propose that we …/Our proposal is to …
- I'd suggest that you reconsider your proposal. After all, …

b. Expressing your opinion

- In my opinion, it would be beneficial to …
- I take the view that, …
- Personally, I think/don't think …
- I am inclined to say …
- As I see the issue …

c. Clarifying your position

- To clarify, what this means is that …
- Allow me to explain …
- I think the key issue/question here is …
- Put differently/another way, we mean/want/plan …

d. Providing additional support for your position

- Let me add that …
- Another point worth mentioning is …
- Also, please keep in mind that …
- As you can see from the company's financial statements …
- The company's financial history provides support for …
- I'd particularly like to stress/emphasize that …

e.   *Summarizing your position*

- At the end of the day …
- The take-away/take-home from this is … (US only)
- To sum up, …
- As I mentioned previously …
- I'd like to reiterate that it is crucial for us to …

f.   *Concluding the negotiations*

- We appreciate your efforts/your cooperation.
- We're happy with that.
- I think that is about as far as we can go on this issue/question.
- I will talk to my client and see what I can do.
- We're hopeful that we can reach a resolution once you take this back to your client.
- We look forward to hearing from you once your client has considered our proposal.
- I look forward to doing business with you in the future.

B.   Questions for the other party to the Negotiation

a.   *Requesting clarification*

- Could you clarify the first point please, I'm not sure I understand/ follow you.
- Could you tell me again why …
- Let's just run through/hit the main points again.
- What is your client's position on …?

b.   *Requesting confirmation*

- Am I understanding you correctly, that …?
- Let me get this straight. Are you proposing that …?
- Are you basically saying that …?
- So, to confirm, we've agreed/your client will agree to …

2

C.   Responding to the other Party

a.   Expressing agreement/responding favorably

- I agree, you are absolutely right.
- We are on the same page here.
- We could live with that.
- I think my client will be amenable to that.
- That is certainly a step into the right direction.

b.   Expressing partial agreement

- That may well be true, but we also have to consider/think about/look at …
- I see your point. However/That said, …
- True, but that is only one side of the issue …
- We're willing to compromise on this issue, but/if …

c.   Expressing disagreement/rejecting a proposal

- I am afraid that is out of the question.
- Unfortunately, I have to disagree with you/we cannot agree to/cannot go along with …
- With all due respect, I don't agree/I don't share your view that …
- With all due respect, the information you have is incorrect.
- We understand your concern, but …
- That would be difficult for us.
- We are not in a position to agree to that.

d.   Withholding information

- I am sorry, but this is confidential information.
- I apologize, but I am not authorized to discuss that information/that issue.
- Sorry, but I am not in a position to answer that question/provide that information.

Personal Notes _____

_____

_____

_____

_____

_____

_____

_____

3 Negotiation Checklist

This legal manual provides an outline for your use in preparing for a negotiation session. Keep in mind that this checklist is by no means intended as a full compendium on negotiation strategy or tactics. There are numerous approaches to negotiation strategy, and countless books and articles on the topic. By contrast, this manual, in keeping with the Legal English Manual's stated goal of serving as a practice-oriented, quick-reference handbook, is designed only to help guide you in preparing for, conducting, and following up on a negotiation. Throughout the checklist, the term "you" refers not only to you as the negotiating party, but also to the client or other party on whose behalf you are negotiating.

The first section, "Pre-Negotiation Considerations," outlines the information and questions with which you should be absolutely familiar before entering into a negotiation, as well as strategic issues to consider in advance.

The second section, "During the Negotiation," briefly addresses strategies to negotiate effectively, as well as administrative considerations that will help you to use your time efficiently.

The third section, "Post-Negotiation Considerations," addresses points for follow-up to ensure that the results you achieve during a negotiation session ultimately lead to the desired outcome.

A.   Pre-Negotiation Considerations

a.   Relationships

* Do you have an existing personal relationship with the other party to the negotiation?
  - how important is this personal relationship to you?
  - how and to what degree will a successful negotiation impact this personal relationship? How and to what degree will an unsuccessful negotiation impact the relationship?
* Do you have an existing business relationship with the other party to the negotiation?
  - how important is this business relationship to you?
  - how and to what degree will a successful negotiation impact this business relationship? How and to what degree will an unsuccessful negotiation impact the relationship?
* Does the current negotiation involve a single transaction, or do you anticipate that it will or could be one in an ongoing series of negotiations on different transactions?

3

b.   *Issues subject to negotiation – your interests and goals*

- Identify each individual issue you intend to address in the negotiation.
- Identify the scope of your authority to negotiate and reach a binding agreement on each issue, and know exactly where the limits lie.
- For issues on which your authority to negotiate is limited (or issues you did not expect to arise during the negotiation), determine in advance how you will handle a negotiation scenario in which your counterpart offers a proposal that exceeds your negotiating authority.
  - Will your client be available by telephone?
  - Do you have any discretion to offer a non-binding counterproposal, on the condition that your client must subsequently approve such a proposal?
  - If you have reached the limits of your negotiating authority on a deal-breaking issue, will it be productive to continue the negotiation on other issues, or should you continue the discussions at a later date when you have obtained further guidance from your client?
  - For each issue, make sure you identify the interest driving your position on that issue, i.e. why are you taking a particular position on that issue. Thoroughly understanding not only your side's positions, but also the rationales underlying these positions will allow you to negotiate more convincingly. In addition, understanding the underlying reasoning for the position you take on each issue will help you, if necessary, to find more creative alternative solutions that differ from your original proposals but nonetheless satisfy your interests.
- In writing, rank each issue by importance and priority to you.
  - Which issues involve your must-have goals, or deal-breakers, and on which issues might you be willing to compromise?
- For issues on which you may be able to compromise, identify the extent to which you can offer a compromise while still satisfying your interests.
  - To ensure that you do not overlook potentially acceptable options during the negotiation, outline, in advance, one or more potential ways in which you could offer a compromise on those issues which matter less to you.
- Identify which issues are related to one another, to what extent, and in what way.
  - Assess how you may be able to present related issues as an attractive "package" in the negotiation.

- Identify other factors that may influence your negotiating positions, particularly where your counterpart knows about and may attempt to use these factors as leverage. Examples include market stability or instability, foreseeable economic changes, financial factors, issues relating to staffing and personnel, deadlines, or existing legal challenges.
    – Determine whether and how you may want to address these additional factors to influence the course of the negotiation.
    – Identify whether and how your counterpart may want to address these additional factors, and determine how you will respond.

c.   *Issues subject to negotiation – the other party's interests and goals*

- Consider whether your counterpart may be likely to raise issues that you do not consider relevant to the negotiation.
    – Make sure you understand why you do not consider these issues relevant.
    – Analyze where your counterpart's interests lie with regard to these issues.
    – Formulate a strategy ahead of time on how to respond if your counterpart raises one or more issues you do not consider relevant.
- For each issue you intend to address in the negotiation, identify what you think your counterpart's position and goals are likely to be, as well as the interests behind these goals. As is true for understanding the interests behind your own goals, understanding why your counterpart sees an issue a particular way will enable you to propose creative alternative solutions to which both parties may be amenable.
- Identify the importance and priority you think your counterpart will assign to each issue.
    – Which issues are likely to be your counterpart's deal-breakers, and on which issues might your counterpart be willing to compromise?
    – If your counterpart is willing to compromise on one or more issues, what can you offer in return?

- Identify other factors that may influence your counterpart's negotiating positions, particularly where you can use these factors as leverage, e.g. market stability or instability, foreseeable economic changes, financial factors, issues relating to staffing and personnel, deadlines, or existing legal challenges.
  - Determine whether and how you may want to address these additional factors to influence the course of the negotiation.

d.   *Best Alternative to a Negotiated Agreement (BATNA)*

- Keep in mind that you do not necessarily have to reach an agreement with your counterpart. How important it is to actually achieve a final agreement in a negotiation will depend on your BATNA – if the negotiations fail, what are your options?
  - Assessing your BATNA requires, yet again, a thorough understanding of the business, personal, legal, and any other interests driving your negotiating positions. Knowing what your true interests are will allow you to identify other options that might serve your interests even if the current negotiations do not result in a productive outcome.
  - The more alternatives you can muster, and the stronger your BATNA is, the less pressure and the more power you will enjoy during the negotiation.
- Analyze your counterpart's BATNA in light of the interests underlying his or her negotiating positions.
  - Assess how strong your counterpart's BATNA and other alternative options are relative to your own.

B.   **During the Negotiation**

1. Administrative and logistical issues

- Make sure the negotiating room is comfortable, that there is ample room for documents, and that water, coffee, and tea are available.
- Make sure you have any necessary documents with you, as well as copies.
- Ask whether your counterpart has any time restrictions, and mention any time restrictions you may have.
- Introduce yourself to anyone you do not yet know, and make sure everyone who has appeared on your counterpart's behalf knows the name and role of any team member accompanying you.

2. Take charge

- After the initial small-talk has subsided, state that you are looking forward to a productive discussion, thus setting a positive, optimistic tone for the negotiation.
- Unless you are in the unlikely situation that you have no information at all regarding your counterpart's negotiating positions, attempt to take charge of the negotiation from the outset.
    - Do not ask for your counterpart's position at the outset.
    - Instead, start by suggesting that you get to the agenda and describe the agenda (as you prepared it).
    - Next, explain your position on the first issue, ideally with a very brief explanation of your underlying interests. State that you believe the position to be fair and reasonable, then say you welcome your opponent's views on how to achieve a mutually agreeable resolution.
- Emphasize subtly how your proposal is to both parties' benefit, referring to your counterpart's goals, and explaining how your proposal will also serve the interests underlying your counterpart's goals.
- Avoid saying "I want" or "I propose." Instead, say "our client," the client's name, or simply "we."
- Make your client look strong. Your client does not "want," or "wish," or "desire." Rather, your client "proposes," "suggests," "takes the view that," "believes that [...] would be a successful and agreeable resolution for all parties," or (if you want to send a very strong message) "expects."
- If your counterpart consistently interrupts you, do not be afraid to point out that the constant interruptions are impeding the progress of the discussion.

3. Emphasize your cooperativeness

- If the tenor of the conversation allows for a personal touch, refer to the productive existing relationship between the parties, or express your ongoing enthusiasm for a future relationship.
- Emphasize that your client has made concessions in the past, has been patient or willing to compromise, and is willing to consider alternative arrangements (as long as they are commercially feasible).

3. Circle back and recap your progress

- At certain intervals, usually after you have finished discussing a particular issue, stop to summarize any progress you have made so far and to recap any agreements you have reached.
- Write down these points of agreement for use in your post-negotiation follow-up.
- Take breaks periodically, and suggest (politely) how long each break should last.

4. Wrap up the negotiation

- When the parties have reached an agreement, or the negotiations have reached what one or both parties consider a natural stopping point, suggest that you summarize once more which issues you have been able to resolve.
- After summarizing any agreements you reached during the negotiation, suggest that you will draft the appropriate agreement and circulate it to all parties by a particular date.
- Identify any additional documents or information you will need, or which you have agreed to send. Set firm deadlines for transmitting this information.
- Thank your counterpart for his or her time and the productive negotiation.

C.   Post-Negotiation Considerations

- If you are negotiating on behalf of a client, inform the client as soon as you can of the negotiation's outcome.
- Assuming you and your counterpart reached an agreement on one or more essential issues, draft an email or a letter as soon as you can setting forth the key points you discussed during the negotiation. Explain that you are preparing a written agreement, and state when you intend to circulate the draft.
- Circulate the draft agreement by or before the deadline you set during or shortly after the negotiation.

4 Client Interview – Phrases and Expressions

The initial client interview serves three main goals: (1) developing a rapport with the client to serve as the basis for the working relationship; (2) gathering all relevant facts; and (3) identifying the main legal issues.

A. Introduction and Preliminary Information

a. *Greeting the client*

- It is a pleasure to meet you (if you have never met the client before)/to meet you in person (if you have previously communicated by email or telephone)/see you (if you have met the client before).
- Thank you for coming to meet with us today.
- Please have a seat.
- Would you like a cup of coffee or some water?
- Our receptionist will provide you with a parking voucher.

b. *Preliminary information*

- Let me give you an overview of what I'd like to discuss with you/cover/ address today.
- I'd like to discuss with you how I can help you achieve your objectives.
- I anticipate that our meeting will last about an hour. Do you have any time restriction?
- I'll ask you some questions about the matter so I can obtain the full picture.
- I will be taking some notes for the file.
- Let me assure you that everything we discuss today will be confidential.
- I have asked my associate, [*name*], to join today's meeting, as he/she will be working on this matter with me.
- Before we start, do you have any questions for me?

4

B. Collecting Information

a. Confirming the accuracy of existing information

- As I understood from your email/our telephone conversation, …
- Based on what you've told me, the main facts are …
- Is it correct that …?
- My understanding of the matter is that … Can you confirm that this is correct?
- I would like to clarify …
- I would like to confirm that the facts, as I currently understand them, are accurate.

b. Gathering additional information

- Tell me what brings you here today, and how I can help you.
- Let's start from the beginning. Tell me …
- As I understand it, … Can you tell me what happened next/what you did next/what the next step was?
- Could you describe the circumstances of the accident/event/ transaction/dispute for me in detail?
- For each step: who was involved/who performed …/who knew about …?
- Do you have anything to add/am I missing any of the salient facts/is there anything else I should know?

c. Reviewing and confirming your understanding of the new information

- So, if I understand you correctly, you are saying that …
- Let me repeat what I understand from you to be the situation/the key issue(s)/the main concern(s).
- So, to reiterate, …
- Allow me to summarize what you have told me.
- Based on what you've told me, am I correct in assuming that …?

C. Providing your Assessment and Legal Advice

a. Identifying and discussing the legal issues

- Based on what you've told me, I see the following main legal issues: …
- The key legal issue here is …
- This means that you may be able to recover damages/sue for breach of contract/bring a claim under the … section of the agreement.
- Under the law, you have a duty to …, which means that …
- Given the circumstances, I think you have a reasonable chance of prevailing here.
- Given the facts, you may face an uphill battle with/in this argument/ this case/this matter, because …
- The law imposes a three-part test in circumstances like these. The three prongs of this test are … This means that we will have to show you can satisfy all three prongs.

b. Providing options and recommendations

- We have a number of legal options/several avenues for resolution here. Based on what you've told me, I would recommend that …
- There are several ways we could proceed, depending on your objectives/ your risk tolerance/your relationship with …
- You are in somewhat of a difficult situation/a tight spot/a quandary/a complicated situation here. I would suggest …, because …
- I think you have a good chance of convincing the court that/reaching a favorable resolution, as …
- This may be a good case in which to consider a settlement, because …
- If you choose to go this route, we would have to …
- Please keep in mind that these options reflect my preliminary assessment. I have to review the documents/the contract in more detail.
- I will have to review … before I can make any legal recommendation. Can you send me a copy of … by tomorrow afternoon?
- I suggest … If you agree, I will draft a settlement agreement/prepare a response to the claims/draft correspondence to opposing counsel/ proceed with the strategy we've discussed.
- Once we …, it will take several weeks until …

4

D.   Concluding the Client Interview

a.   *Addressing next steps*

- What do you think/how does this sound to you?
- I will prepare/draft …
- I will circulate the documents to my team, and we will prepare/draft …
- We will go ahead with the research we discussed and prepare a detailed analysis of the law on …
- I will call you in the next week to give you an update.
- I will most certainly keep you informed of any developments.

b.   *Contact information*

- This is my business card, please call me anytime.
- The best way to reach me is generally …
- What is the best way to reach you?
- Do you prefer email or the telephone?

c.   *Finishing the interview*

- Thank you for the opportunity/I appreciate the opportunity to work on this case.
- Thank you for entrusting us with this case.
- We will be very pleased to handle this matter for you.
- Please call me anytime if you have any questions at all.

"There are several ways we could proceed, depending on your risk tolerance..."

5   Client Interview – Checklist

This legal manual provides an outline for use in preparing for an initial client interview. The first section, "Before the Interview" identifies information you should know inside and out so you have it at your fingertips during the interview. This section also addresses administrative aspects of planning the interview.

The second section, "Conducting the Interview" addresses considerations for structuring the interview in an efficient and productive manner.

The third section, "After the Interview" addresses points for follow-up.

A.   Before the Interview

a.   Scope of the representation

- Type of case and exact client(s) (e.g. do you represent only the corporate entity, or also any officers, directors, or employees?)
- Fee agreement, any alternative billing arrangements (e.g. flat-fee for the matter, flat fees for certain portions of the matter, contingency fee [in the US only], partial contingency fee [in the US only])
- Matter staffing (which partners and/or associates, fee schedules for each)
- Check for any conflicts of interest, obtain conflict waivers if necessary
- Estimated budget for fees and any other anticipated costs (if you have previously discussed fees with the client, or if the client has asked for an estimate)

b.   Information regarding the client

- Corporate clients: name, entity type, major divisions within the company, contact person
- Nature of client's business
- Client's ownership structure
- Main competitors, litigation history
- Client's financial situation (e.g. stock price, quarterly or annual statements if the client is a publicly listed company)

- Individual clients: name(s), contact information, family status (e.g. marital status, dependents), general financial situation, any special issues (citizenship, religion, illness)
- Client's familiarity, if any, with the relevant law
- Client's primary objectives in retaining (UK: instructing) you
- Source of client referral (e.g. colleague, other client or professional contact)

c. Matter status

aa) Facts
- Summary of available facts you have already received from the client or other sources
- Summary of any preliminary factual research
- List of additional factual information you require
- List of relevant documents (a) you have and (b) you need

bb) Legal issues
- Preliminary analysis identifying key legal issues and relevant law
- Preliminary analysis of possible approaches or avenues for resolutions
- Any relevant legal research memoranda
- Any previous legal advice provided to the client (by you or by other counsel)

d. Case management and relevant deadlines
- List of all known deadlines relating to the matter
- Anticipated timeline for handling matter (distinguish between "hard" deadlines, which you cannot extend, and "soft" deadlines, which are more flexible)

e. Administrative and logistical issues
- Confirm the date, time, and location of the meeting in an email to the client
- Confirm that your administrative assistant has reserved a conference room
- Identify all individuals participating in the meeting (on client's and on lawyer's side)
- Identify any tasks for the client (e.g. signing documents, providing documents)

- Confirm that the signed Letter of Engagement is in the file
- Confirm that a copy of the Fee Agreement is in the file
- For a pitch to potential clients: bring brochures or other information regarding the law firm, information on similar matters your firm has handled successfully, and copies of the bios for all lawyers you plan to staff on the matter

B.   Conducting the Interview

a.   *Beginning the interview*

- After greeting the client(s) and introducing any colleagues also attending the meeting, provide a brief overview of the goals for the meeting
- Ask whether the client has any initial administrative questions for you
- Ask whether the client has any time restrictions for the meeting
- Mention the attorney-client privilege to put the client at ease and to encourage the client to be forthcoming in providing information
- Identify any tasks for the client (e.g. signing documents) upfront

b.   *Objectives of the interview*

aa)   From the lawyer's perspective

- Demonstrating that you are the right lawyer to hire for the matter
- Getting to know your client and his or her preferences (e.g. how he/she likes to communicate, does/he she seem to enjoy pleasantries or getting straight to the point, how cost-sensitive is he/she, how hands-on and involved does he/she want to be)
- Understanding the client's problem(s), goals, and any other issues
- Creating realistic expectations with regard to the outcome of the matter and to costs
- Identifying any possible ethical issues and communicating these to the client
- Collecting all facts you will need for your analysis
- Presenting your initial assessment of options for handling the matter

bb)   From the client's perspective

- Feeling confident that he/she has hired a knowledgeable, ethical, and efficient lawyer

- Understanding his/her options, and being in a position to make an informed decision on how to proceed

c.   *Gathering facts*

- Briefly outline the facts as you know them, and ask the client to confirm their accuracy
- Explain generally what you need to know, and what is not important
- Working in chronological or thematic order, ask the client to fill in any gaps
- Use open-ended questions (e.g. "What happened next?") initially rather than yes-no questions
- Use yes-no questions to confirm particular facts, or if there are only a few additional details you still need
- Keep a running list of any facts you need which the client does not know, or of any questions for which you or the client will determine the answers at a later point
- Periodically ask the client: "is that correct," "am I missing anything," "do I have the chronology correct," or "do you have anything to add to that?"
- If time permits, run through a brief summary of the new facts you obtained at the end of the interview

d.   *Providing your preliminary legal assessment*

- Identify what law applies
- Identify and explain the key legal issues
- Provide your preliminary legal assessment, including alternative possibilities for resolution, with a concise benefit and risk assessment for each option
- Periodically ask the client: "does that make sense?" or "do you have any questions so far?"

e.   *Determining the next steps*

- Discuss with the client how attractive he/she finds each of the options you've presented, and how risk-averse he/she is, to determine your course of action
- Identify any upcoming deadlines, and explain what you or the client will have to do to meet each one

- Propose concrete next steps, and confirm that the client would like you to proceed
- Identify any other resources you may need (e.g. expert witnesses, accountants, tax specialists, colleagues who can provide additional insight or additional legal services)
- Propose a time for the next client meeting or telephone call, and identify what you will accomplish in the meantime
- Ask again whether the client has any questions for you, or whether the client is unclear on any issues you discussed during the meeting

C.   After the Interview

a.   Tasks for your team

- Place your meeting notes in the client's file
- Prepare a to-do list and assign lawyers on your team to each task
- Prepare a timeline for each task on your to-do list
- Prepare any follow-up communication to the client
- Calendar (UK: schedule) and prepare for the next client meeting

b.   Follow-up with the client

- Prepare email correspondence to the client (a) thanking the client for his/her time, (b) stating that you appreciate the client's trust and the chance to handle the matter, and (c) briefly outlining the next steps upon which you agreed during the meeting
- Send the client any documents he/she should see or asked to see
- Follow up with the client on any documents he/she agreed to provide to you
- Follow up with the client on any facts or other information he/she agreed to provide to you
- Confirm the date and time of the next meeting

6 Proposals – Responding to an RFP

Rather than simply retaining a single trusted law firm to handle their legal work, clients are increasingly choosing to issue Requests for Proposals (RFPs) to an array of law firms. In a process colloquially known by the derogatory term "beauty contest," which is a bid for the client's legal work, each law firm will provide and frequently also present a proposal for legal services. The client will then choose the proposal which best suits its needs with regard to hiring new counsel. For this reason, lawyers need the skills to prepare a compelling, competitive proposal document, including choosing appropriate content and determining what the client is looking for in a proposal document. This manual describes the essential considerations applicable (1) to the pre-proposal phase and (2) to preparing and presenting the proposal itself.

A.   Pre-Proposal Phase

The *pre-proposal phase* involves starting to prepare a proposal and making some seminal decisions. First, run a conflicts check in your firm's conflicts database. Make sure to run conflicts on the client's full corporate name, any short form names the client uses, the names of all partners, officers, directors, and other senior management, and alternative spellings of these names to capture possible misspellings in your database.

Second, once you confirm that the potential new client has cleared conflicts, check if there is a way to obtain the legal work in question without submitting a proposal. Maybe you can convince the client that your firm is the right choice without going out to tender. Ideally, you or someone on your team will have a personal connection with the client. Alternatively, you may know that another client of yours (with whom you have a good relationship) has an excellent connection to your new client and can put in a word for you. Either way, good relationships are key, as is true in general when working with clients.

Third, barring such an option, if the client decides to go ahead with the proposal process, you will receive an RFP formally (via an official RFP letter) or informally (e.g. orally). Either way, make sure you acknowledge receipt of the RFP within the next 24 hours. Then start planning. Often, the client will expect your proposal within a time frame as short as

48 hours. Moreover, you will have to prepare and write your proposal in addition to your billable work.

Fourth, several people are usually involved in preparing a proposal, and they may not all see eye to eye at the outset. Things can get hectic quickly, so having a solid strategy in advance is essential. To avoid forgetting items or spending too much time on one-step and running into time constraints, (1) set up a timeline immediately and (2) identify a project manager in charge of the entire process.

In addition, consider the following issues crucial to this phase:
- Do we actually want this matter?
- Is it in line with our firm's primary areas of work?
- Is there a positional conflict? (For example, firms that handle mostly defense work will often be hesitant to accept plaintiff-side matters, lawyers who represent insurers generally do not represent insurees, and franchisor-side lawyers generally do not represent franchisees even if no actual conflict of interest exists.)
- Is the proposal realistic? Can we win this matter?
- Is it worth it from a financial and resource perspective?
- How can we staff this team effectively?
- Do we have lawyers with the right expertise?
- Do we have the capacity to handle this matter?
- Conduct background research on the client, its decision makers, and its competitors.
- Recognize and make sure you understand the client's business needs.
- Start capturing ideas, solutions, benefits, available evidence, and competitive differentiators, i.e. what makes you different from, i.e. better than your competitors.

Tip:

Consider early on how to actually put together the proposal document. Alert your document manager and/or designers of the upcoming assignment. Work with them to understand the processes involved and meet deadlines. Ensure a fail-safe delivery – you haven't come this far to be eliminated because your proposal is late.

Some firms also have a strict policy on when to say no, i.e. when not to bid:
- *NO prior existing relationship with the potential new client*
- *NO access to decision makers*
- *NO advance notice of RFP*
- *NO time/resources to respond appropriately*

6

B.   Preparing and Presenting the Proposal

Once you have decided to participate in the RFP process, start setting up the proposal document. If the client has given you a structure in its RFP, then follow that structure. If the RFP provides no particular order or structure, choose the following approach:

a.   *Cover letter*

- The cover letter is the first thing your client will read. Therefore, it should contain a summary of your most important points. Write in an enthusiastic style, and convey your two to three key messages clearly.
- If you also write an executive summary, make your cover letter short to avoid duplication.
- If you do not write an executive summary, use the cover letter to demonstrate your understanding of the client's legal needs, challenges, and strategic goals. Also address – in an abbreviated form – how you might approach finding solutions.
- As is true for the executive summary, write the cover letter at the end, after you have written the entire proposal document.
- The cover letter should not exceed two pages.

b.   *Table of contents*

- Confirm with the client whether your proposal should follow the structure of the client's RFP. Adjusting your proposal to the RFP often makes it easier for the client to compare the proposals it receives.
- If you are in a position to choose a structure yourself, use the one in this book (a-i).
- Start each chapter on a new page.

c.   *Executive summary*

- Link the client's goals to your solutions, and demonstrate how your solutions contribute to the client's overall mission.
- Where possible, introduce the client's hot button issues using its own words and terms. The order of priority should reflect the client's needs and key aspects of your proposal.
- Create a sub-section for each hot button issue. Under each such issue, set out your solution to the client's needs, including the solu-

tion's benefits and features, and proof of your experience and success handling similar issues. Prominently tie in major differentiators.

- Close with a summary of your proposal, including the unique contribution your solution will make to the client's success. Summarize your fees and added value components. Conclude by clearly stating the next step(s) you recommend.

- If the set-up of your document is not obvious, preview how your proposal is organized for the client's convenience and easy evaluation. For example, you can insert a list explaining that "your question on […] is answered in section […], chapter […] on page […]."

d.   *How your approach aligns with the RFP*

- Reinforce your understanding of the client's legal needs, motivators, and hot button issues by quoting the client or extracting relevant excerpts from the client's own material. Phrase your message in the client's own words. Show you have done your homework.

e.   *Testimonials, case studies, and other secondary evidence*

- While highlighting your capabilities is good, providing evidence is even better to show that you have successfully handled similar matters in the past. Case studies and testimonials are two of the most effective ways to underscore your track record of success. Your *case studies* should address any previous experience with the new client, your experience with similar engagements (similar projects for clients in a different industry), and your experience working with similar organizations (clients in the same industry as the new client). You should focus on positive outcomes and value you delivered.

- Your *testimonials* let other clients speak for you. Think carefully about whom you would like to include in this portion of your proposal. What is the relationship between your client and the person giving a recommendation? Consider providing the person giving the testimonial a short list of bullet points on which the testimonial could or should focus, or even suggested phrases that you might like the testimonial to include. Be sure to ask your recommender in advance whether he or she would be comfortable receiving suggestions of this nature from you.

Apart from case studies and testimonials, your proposal can also tie in the following aspects:

- Industry knowledge/specialists on your team
- Technical knowledge/specialists on your team
- References
- Awards
- Knowledge management and sources
- Technology to assist you in handling the matter
- Thought leadership
- Networks
- Professional development

f.   *Staffing your team*

- You have limited space, so carefully select the most relevant information to include in your bio overview, based on the client's legal needs, wants, and evaluation criteria.
- For each team member, include the following information:
  - Value/commitment statement – what value will this person add for the client?
  - Role – what will his or her role be in this engagement?
  - Relevant experience – what client-relevant experience does this person possess?
  - Testimonials – let your clients speak for you.

g.   *Fees*

- How much are we prepared to invest now in light of future returns?
- Address fees early and review them throughout the bid. Moving early enables the team to test the client's budget and cost-sensitivity.

h.   *References*

- Make sure your references follow a clear and logic sequence.
- Consider references in the same industry, as well as references related to similar projects.

i.   *Appendix*

- Use appendices to streamline your proposal.
- Content of interest to most evaluators should go in the body of the proposal document; content of interest to one or a few evaluators should go in an appendix.
- Include detailed information in the appendices, e.g. full bios, detail on approach or methodology, your product and services, and your capabilities, as well as thought leadership and knowledge tools (e.g. websites, blogs, intranet resources, pod casts, newsletters, and other tools that support personal and group knowledge sharing).
- Refer to all appendices in the main body of your proposal.
- If an appendix is extensive, provide an introductory paragraph that summarizes the key points and provides a roadmap of the content.

Proposal wording:

Proposal	also referred to as an offer, bid, or tender. A proposal is a written offer from a seller to a prospective buyer.
Executive Summary	a short summary of the offer's main points intended for the senior level decision makers in the client's organization.
Hot Button Issues	singularly important issue or set of issues likely to drive decisions.
RFP	Request for Proposal = a client document requesting a proposal.
Value Proposition	a promise of value to be delivered. It is the primary reason a prospective client should choose your legal services.

7

7   Presentations – Checklist with Specific Pointers on Pitches

Oral presentations are an important but frequently underestimated step in the proposal or pitching process. To set yourself up for success, make sure you set aside plenty of time. You will be surprised at how much time preparing and rehearsing your presentation will take. In preparing your presentation, start by taking the following preliminary points into consideration:

- *Who will be attending from the client's side?*
- *Whom will we send?*
- *Who will be presenting on what topic(s)?*
- *Which questions could the client ask during the presentation?*
- *How will we answer these questions?*

A.   Preparing for your Presentation

The oral presentation gives you the chance to reinforce your key propositions and present yourself and your colleagues as an effective team. Performing well in an oral presentation will often cement a favorable decision the client has already made, and may even turn the tide in your favor if a client is on the fence about hiring you. A poor presentation, however, can blow your chances, so careful preparation and full rehearsals are vital.

Start developing your approach to the oral presentation well before submitting your proposal. Ask yourself questions such as:

- To whom are you going to present?
- What does the room where you will present look like?
- How will you handle introductions?
  - Will one team member introduce everyone on the team, or will each team member introduce himself or herself?
  - In what order will team members be introduced?

- Who will address which topic(s), and who will answer which question(s)?
- How will you deal with objections or questions to which you do not know the answer?
- How will you close your presentation?
- What will your next steps be?

B.   Introduction to the Presentation

The first few seconds of a meeting can be crucial to the entire business relationship. Think about it: you never get a second chance to make a first impression. The lead-in to a business conversation when you first meet the client, before you actually start presenting, often involves small talk. Keep in mind that it's the first impression that counts, and how you handle small talk can make or break the client's first impression of you!

The goals of small talk are to:
- establish a personal rapport when you first meet the client
- make the client feel comfortable and valued at the outset
- engage in a casual, entertaining chat about something positive. In so doing, you forge your image as an optimistic, self-confident, and outgoing person.

The most difficult thing about small talk is taking the first step, i.e. choosing a topic. Topics **appropriate** for small talk include:
- the weather
- traveling/your commute
- current events (positive ones)
- holidays/seasons
- personal interests/hobbies
- arts/culture
- food/drink

Avoid topics such as:
- politics
- money
- personal problems
- religion

In addition to the topic or topics you choose for small talk, focus on the non-verbal aspects of your initial meeting with the client. Typically, well over half of communication happens non-verbally. Pay attention to non-verbal cues such as your client's facial expressions, gestures, posture, and voice. Further, be sure to smile! People with a genuine smile are perceived as being not only more honest but more competent than those who do not smile or whose facial expressions indicate dissatisfaction.

C. During the Presentation

The best way to ace your presentation is to practice your delivery out loud in advance, ideally with an audience who can provide constructive criticism where necessary. In addition, the following pointers will help you score points with your audience:

- Show enthusiasm. Be excited about what you present by using open body language, smiling, and speaking in a friendly, enthusiastic tone of voice.
- Speak up and speak clearly. Both will make you appear confident. Use your voice to emphasize important points.
- Make eye-contact with your audience and hold it.
- Watch your body language when other presenters on your team are speaking.
- Rather than rushing through your presentation, make a conscious effort to speak slowly and deliberately.
- Pause from time to time to vary your rhythm and to emphasize or reinforce a point. A short pause can give your audience time to digest and reflect upon your words, as well as lending you authority and creating an impact.
- Pay attention to your gestures and avoid gestures below your waist.
- Show that you are enjoying yourself.
- Be yourself, rather than trying to act like someone you definitely are not.

Finally, as a substantial proportion of our communication is non-verbal, what matters is not only WHAT we say but especially HOW we say something. To this end, make sure that the audience can easily follow your presentation's central theme.

If you decide to use visual aids, make sure they help the audience remember your key messages. As the purpose of a visual aid is to make an impact on your audience, visual aids should not serve as a simple crutch to aid you in giving your presentation. Nor should visual aids be so self-explanatory or so distracting that they draw the audience's attention away from you. For that reason, a straightforward, simple visual aid to which you can refer while developing your main points will be most effective. Keep the following pointers in mind when using visual aids:

- Keep visual aids simple and clear.
- Use images to reinforce your messages and make them memorable.
- Ensure consistency of style, syntax, and grammar throughout the presentation.
- Avoid using excessive color.
- Avoid complex and overcrowded layouts.
- Avoid long lists of bullet points.
- Avoid making text too small, crowded, or illegible.

D.   Handling Q&A

A successful presentation prompts questions from the audience, so you have to be prepared. Think of each question as an opportunity to make a positive statement. Decide in advance how you will handle questions:

- Determine who will answer which questions from the audience.
- Respond to answers directly and without delay.
- Place key messages liberally during the Q&A as well as during the body of your presentation.
- Do not become defensive. Acknowledge the question or comment and give your answer in a neutral manner.
- Prepare at least two questions to ask your audience.

E.   After the Presentation

Particularly in situations where you are offering a proposal, your work does not end once the presentation is over, despite the relief you may feel after a successful presentation. Situations in which the client confirms its intent to hire you directly after your presentation are exceedingly rare. As a result, it is essential that you follow up with key decision makers for the client to make sure the client has all the information it needs, and that your competition has not raised any other issues you did not have a chance to address.

In addition, once you are aware of the client's decision, conduct a debriefing session.

- Win or lose, you should debrief the client:
  - How did you perform against your competitors?
  - Why did you win or lose the bid?
  - How can you improve the next time around?
  - How did the client perceive your team?
- A neutral person, i.e. someone who was not on the team, should conduct the debriefing.
- Identify opportunities to develop future relationships with the client.
- Hold an internal debriefing session with your team to discuss any lessons you learned and how you will handle similar presentations going forward.

8 Job Interview – Phrases and Expressions

A. Introduction

- Thank you for inviting me to interview for the [*Associate/Trainee/ Corporate/Tax*] position.
- I am excited about the opportunity to interview for a position with your firm's [*Corporate Law/Taxation/Real Estate*] group.
- I am eager/excited/enthusiastic to learn more about the job opportunity and your firm.
- I learned/heard about this opportunity through your posting on the firm's website/from [*name of person or recruiting agency*].

B. Explaining your Interest in the Position

a. *I am very interested in working for your firm/ company because …*

- the firm offers its lawyers the opportunity to …
- I am impressed by the firm's commitment to …
- the firm offers the challenging and rewarding substantive work experience for which I am looking.
- this position provides the dynamic team environment and complex cases I enjoy.

b. *I am interested in working in [area of law] because …*

- I am enthusiastic about …/I am eager to …
- I enjoy the intellectual challenges of …
- I think working on cases involving [*details of area of law*] is fascinating.
- I find it very rewarding to provide my clients with an understanding of the laws and procedures affecting them and their business dealings.
- I plan/intend/aim to become a specialist in [*area of law*].

C. Explaining why you should be hired

- I believe I am a good fit for this position because …
- My work experience and my interest in … qualify me well for this position.
- I am confident I can contribute to/be an asset to your firm because …
- My background and my work ethic would allow me to serve your clients well, as …
- The position suits both my background and my interests well, because …
- I have extensive knowledge in [area of law].
- I have substantial experience with …
- As a result of [education/prior work experience], I have expertise in …
- My skillset provides a good match for the position because …
- Through my work/studies in …, I developed strong analytical skills.
- My ability to multi-task successfully allows me to work well under pressure.
- I am a strong team player.
- I enjoy taking on leadership roles and taking ownership of projects, for example …
- I am passionate about …

D. Discussing your Background and Skillset

a. Legal education

- I studied law at the university of [city] and graduated in [year].
- I obtained my Master's degree in [date].
- I passed the bar exam in [state/jurisdiction] in [year] …
- I graduated with Honors in [subject]. (US only)
- I was a teaching assistant/research assistant to a Professor of [area of law].
- As part of my studies, I took part in an exchange programme with the university of [city], during which I learned …

b.   *Work experience*

- During my studies, I held a summer clerkship/internship in a law firm specializing in [*areas of law*] to gain first-hand experience working in [*area of law*].
- The clerkships/internships provided a tremendous learning experience because ...
- As a result of these clerkships, I developed a strong interest in/passion for [*legal area*]/These clerkships solidified my strong interest in/passion for [*legal area*].
- In my last position with [*name of employer*], I was responsible for ...
- In my previous position, I was in charge of ...
- Through my work for [*name of employer*], I gained significant experience advising clients in [*area of law*].
- In my current position, I have a great deal of autonomy working on ...
- During the last ... years, I specialised in ...

c.   *Language skills*

- My native language is German, but I am also fluent/proficient in ...
- I have a strong/an excellent command of English.
- I recently completed a legal English course in ...
- I intend to take the ILEC exam next year.

E.   Questions for the Interviewer

a.   *Questions about the position*

- How would you describe the key aspects of this position?
- What would my primary areas of responsibility be?
- To what extent would my practice involve ...?
- Would I have the opportunity to specialize in [*area of law*]?
- How much client contact would I have?
- Does the position include cross-border work?
- Does the position offer the opportunity to gain international experience?
- What skills do you believe would be most useful for this position?
- How would you describe the ideal candidate for this position?

b.   Questions about the firm

- Can you explain the firm's partnership track?
- What do you like about the firm's culture?
- Can you describe the firm's management structure for me?
- Can you tell me more about the firm's training program for new lawyers?
- Does the firm offer practical training in [*area of law*] that will allow me to develop additional skills in …?
- What leadership opportunities does the firm offer?
- Are the lawyers in your firm expected to be specialists, or to develop expertise in a broad range of areas of law?
- Can trainee lawyers rotate through several departments to gain exposure to different practice areas?
- Does your firm support business development activities, such as writing on real-estate issues in professional magazines, or participation in local lawyers' organizations?
- What are your firm's working languages?

"Can you tell me more about the firm's legal English training program for new lawyers?"

Authors' Profiles

Kathrin Weston Walsh

- US attorney licensed in the District of Columbia and Colorado.
- J.D., M.A. (Duke University School of Law, Dartmouth College)
- Professional Legal English Language Program Director and Coach for Lawbility, Zurich, Switzerland
- Lecturer in Legal English, University of Lucerne, Switzerland
- Complex Commercial Litigation Attorney, Perkins Coie LLP and Holme Roberts and Owen LLP (now Bryan Cave LLP)

Julian Cornelius

- US attorney licensed in the state of New York, Solicitor licensed in Ireland, England and Wales, accredited Mediator
- LL.M. (University College Dublin), LL.B (Griffith College Dublin)
- Founder of The Legal Beagle (Brazil), providing services for lawyers, law students and other professionals with requirements in Legal English (www.thelegalbeagle.com.br)
- Professional Legal English Language Coach for Lawbility

Jenna Bollag

- Admitted as a Lawyer in the Supreme Court of Victoria, Australia
- BA LL.B (with Honours) (Monash University, Melbourne)
- Legal Counsel in Commercial Law, Dr. J. Bollag & Cie., Zug, Switzerland; Commercial Law Clerk at King & Wood Mallesons, Allens and Arnold Bloch Leibler
- Professional Legal English Language Coach for Lawbility

Sandra Kuhn-Schulthess

- Master's in Law (University of St. Gallen)
- Master of Advanced Studies ZFH in Customer Relationship Management (ZHAW Winterthur)
- Founder and Director of arteverba (www.arteverba.ch)
- Professional Legal English Language Coach for Lawbility

Alison Wiebalck

- Former Solicitor of the Supreme Court of New South Wales
- BA LL.B (Macquarie University, Sydney), Doctor of Laws (UNISA, Pretoria)
- Founder and Director of legalenglishskills.com
- Legal English consultant in Zurich, Switzerland

Richard Norman

- Solicitor of the Supreme Court of England and Wales, LL.B, LL.M. (University College, London), Alfred Beit Scholar
- Vice President, Legal and Corporate Affairs, Dell Inc. from 1993 to 2007
- Consultant for "Lawyers in Business" in London; co-author of "Managing In-House Legal Services" (ISBN 978-3-7255-6252-7); Legal English tutor and law lecturer, Switzerland; consultant for various multinational in-house legal departments

Clemens von Zedtwitz

- Admitted to the bar in Switzerland
- Degrees from the University of St. Gallen and postgraduate degree (LL.M.) from the University of California, Los Angeles (UCLA)

LEGAL ENGLISH PUBLICATIONS BY LAWBILITY

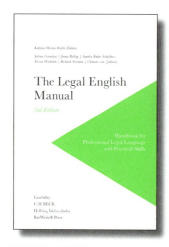

The Legal English Manual

Handbook for Professional Legal
Language and Practice Skills

Kathrin Weston Walsh (Editor)
Julian Cornelius
Jenna Bollag
Sandra Kuhn-Schulthess
Alison Wiebalck
Richard Norman
Clemens von Zedtwitz

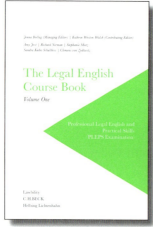

The Legal English Course Book

Volume One
Professional Legal English and
Practical Skills (PLEPS Examination)

Jenna Bollag (Managing Editor)
Kathrin Weston Walsh (Contributing Editor)
Amy Jost
Richard Norman
Stephanie Motz
Sandra Kuhn-Schulthess
Clemens von Zedtwitz

The Legal English Course Book

Volume Two
Professional Legal English and
Practical Skills (PLEPS Examination)

Jenna Bollag (Managing Editor)
Kathrin Weston Walsh (Contributing Editor)
Amy Jost
Richard Norman
Stephanie Motz
Sandra Kuhn-Schulthess
Clemens von Zedtwitz

www.legalenglishexperts.com

LAWBILITY

Praise for the 1st edition

Praise for the 1st edition

❝ I am a practising lawyer in Scotland, as well as a part time lecturer and tutor at the University of Glasgow. This book is an outstanding guide, whether you are a lawyer or not, in informing both students and clients about Legal English and concepts. ❞

Mike Graham | Director Business Law MacRoberts, Solicitors Glasgow & Edinburgh (Scotland)

❝ If you're a legal English teacher and need a course book or supplementary material, the Legal English Manual delivers. From definitions to practical examples, it's a one-stop solution. ❞

Amy Jost | BA/CELTA/SVEB 1/M.S.Ed.
Professional Language Teacher, Talking Heads, Zug (Switzerland)

❝ A major contribution to professional legal English. Every corporate lawyer will need a desk copy. ❞

Sophia Barinova | Ph.D. | Legal English Trainer | Head of the Legal English Centre, Saint Petersburg (Russia) | Senior Lecturer in Legal and Business English, Saint Petersburg University (Russia)

❝ As a Legal English specialist and a teacher, I am always on the lookout for a good reference for my students and for practicing lawyers. The Legal English Manual achieves this purpose elegantly and very practically in four succinctly written parts. The writing in the book practices what it preaches for written and oral legal communication in English: Clarity and Conciseness! It is a compact reference in less than 200 pages and won't take up any space in your briefcase! ❞

Peter K. Cramer | Ph.D., M.A. TESOL (Teaching English to Speakers of Other Languages), LL.M. | Assistant Dean, Washington University School of Law, Saint Louis (USA) | Author of Drafting Contracts in Legal English: Cross-Border Agreements Governed by US Law, Wolters Kluwer, 2013

❝ The Legal English Manual is a valuable tool for foreign lawyers seeking to improve their written and oral English skills. I highly recommend this handbook to all legal practitioners who intend to increase their knowledge and skills within the common law English environment. ❞

Fred Ross III | Esq., MCR | Professor of Law
Handong International Law School (Korea)